Coming of Age: Andy Roddick's Breakthrough Year

Coming of Age: Andy Roddick's Breakthrough Year

Tom & Beth Donelson

iUniverse, Inc.
New York Lincoln Shanghai

Coming of Age: Andy Roddick's Breakthrough Year

iUniverse, Inc.

For information address:
iUniverse, Inc.
2021 Pine Lake Road, Suite 100
Lincoln, NE 68512
www.iuniverse.com

ISBN: 0-595-30785-X

Printed in the United States of America

Contents

Acknowledgements

We would like to acknowledge the following people for their help in writing this book: Greg Starko of the ATP, Scot Hirschfield of SFX, and Natalie Frank of the LoveLady Agency for their help. We would like to thank the Roddick Family for their cooperation and the members of Roddick'n'Roll website including Susan Seemiller, Fiona Simon, Carolyn Austin, Anne Lawrence, Sandra Murphy, Caryn Sweeney, and Laura Gardner for their observations. Also, we can't forget Kat Donelson for her help with the photography. In addition, we appreciate the insight of Jon Wertheim, James Buddell, and Brad Falkner.

Neither Andy Roddick nor the Roddick family have any control over the content contained in, or editing of, this book. To the extent that Andy, his family, and his representatives have assisted in other ways, their help is greatly appreciated.

We also wish to thank Janice Donelson for her patience and willingness on occasion to even join us for our travels to various Tennis events. (Even though she appeared to have a good time.)

Introduction

Tennis is a solitary sport. It is played between the white lines of a rectangular court, and the two players stand alone. No coaches to advise you or encourage you. They are in the stands, watching with the rest of us. No! Tennis is a solitary game. For a Tennis player, his or her failure is out there for the world to see.

Another aspect of Tennis players is that they have to win or at least finish deep in any tournament to make a living. There are no guaranteed contracts. Only the best get extra revenues from Madison Avenue. And, of course, you will not get the big contract without being a winner. Failure is not an option.

Since 1989, Americans have dominated the Tennis world. Pete Sampras was the dominant player in the 90's, basically making Wimbledon his personal playground; and where there was grass or hard court—Pete Sampras was the favorite. When Sampras showed signs of aging over the past three years, Andre Agassi found the fountain of youth. Agassi, who nearly quit Tennis in the mid 90's, created a second career in Tennis. Since 1999, Agassi has won five majors and at the age of 33 is still one of Tennis's best.

The golden age of American Tennis is in transition, and Andy Roddick is considered the next great American hope. Scot Spits of ESPN wrote, "Roddick is a perplexing player, seemingly capable of anything with his powerful serve and a punishing forehand. While he has been seen as a player who thrives on adrenaline, perhaps his mind and game are maturing." Roddick is a 21-year old phenomenon-with 130 mph serves, but who is still trying to develop the complete game. His backhand is still his weakest spot, and in the past, his conditioning was suspect. At least until the 2003 Australian Open.

We suspect that what makes Roddick so appealing is his monster serves. Americans are in love with power and in Roddick, his serve represents the ultimate power in Tennis. There are very few Tennis players that can match Roddick's power in the serve department. Roddick is now working on the complete game.

Roddick's major challenge in 2003 was to establish his own identity. Beginning the year at the tender age of 20, Roddick had American Tennis on his shoulder, a burden not easily borne by most athletes. For Roddick, the comparisons between Sampras and Agassi were and still are constant. When Sampras was Roddick's age, he had already won a major but in the case of Agassi, Andre would not win his first major until he turned 22. Agassi's career nearly ended in the mid 90's, so early stardom proved to be a curse not a blessing. The pressure of being a Tennis poster boy became unbearable, and Agassi almost squandered his opportunities. By the end of 1997, Agassi was not even listed in the top 100 Tennis players, but did manage to retool his game and found himself back on top in short order. Since 1999, Agassi has been the best player at the majors. Sampras and Agassi have snagged 22 majors between them and both men have put their own imprint upon the sport.

That is Roddick's curse—to follow two of America's greatest players. Sampras and Agassi had to pick up the mantle of Jimmy Connors and John McEnroe though there was one difference. By the time that Sampras and Agassi appeared on the Tennis scene, McEnroe had not won a major in six years and Connors was closing in on 40 years of age. Roddick, however, must follow two men who are still winning majors and who are still capable of dominating in the sport. Sampras has won three majors since 1999 and has also appeared in three straight US Opens, this while the Tennis pundits were burying Sampras's career. Agassi managed to win five out of the last eighteen majors that he appeared in. The old lions of American Tennis had yet to give up their mantle and Roddick suffered in comparison. Since 1990, Sampras and Agassi appeared in 32 major finals—winning 22 of them. (In five of those majors, Agassi and Sampras squared off against each other five times with Sampras holding the edge 4-1.) Like Mickey Mantle having to follow the great Joe DiMaggio, Roddick was following two historical figures in the Tennis world. The pressure of being America's future can be awesome, and it does not help that the two players who are America's present Tennis stars still have talent left in the gas tank. This was Roddick's world in January of 2003.

Roddick brings to Tennis one intangible. He brings charisma. Roddick truly enjoys being center stage. His enthusiasm is contagious on the court, and he truly processes rock star status. Our first glimpse of Roddick was at the 2002 Masters event in Cincinnati. Everywhere Roddick went, there were massive followings of fans, many of them female. Being good looking and single are two qualities that Madison Avenue loves and the Tennis world needs. In contrast to Lleyton

Hewitt, who does not appear to love the publicity or headlines, Roddick enjoys being a celebrity. He sells the game of Tennis, and when he takes the next step as a player, he will give Men's Tennis what Serena and Venus give Women's Tennis—a star that transcends the sport and is capable of reaching new fans.

Samantha, from the Ohio Tip Center Tennis team, summed up the feelings of many young teenage girls, "He is really hot." Other ladies of the Tip Center Tennis team added their own comments, "love the visor", "Best server", and "love his clothes." These young ladies spent most of their time watching Roddick practicing before his first match at the 2003 Cincinnati Masters, shrieking and cheering. On one occasion, they yelled in unison, "We love you, Andy!" Andy responded by waving and tipping his hat.

One example of Andy's appeal was reflected in a series of EMAILS after the Australian Open. Tennis is the international sport and the Internet makes it even easier to follow the game. "I just want to congratulate you on your awesome run at the Aussie Open. You just don't know how proud all your fans are."—Margaux, 17, Philippines, was just one message left for Andy on the Roddick'n'Roll website. It is said that the sport is the toy department of American life, and it is through sports that we can see athletes do what is considered impossible and revel in it.

"Absolutely amazing job at the Australian Open. Honestly, the last 2 matches I had tears in my eyes at the end. I'm so unbelievably proud of you. Not just as a tennis player, but as a person as well, you truly have the heart of a champion…Your fan always, Angela" is just one example of how a superstar can garner emotions from the average sport fan. A chat room in any Roddick website just as Roddick'n'Roll features fans from around the world. You will see German spoken as English. It is this devotion that drives sports, for, short of war, sports gives us heroes. When the Williams' sisters play, the ratings go up. Roddick has that potential to take Men's Tennis to new levels.

A second example occurred in 2003, in Houston during a doubles match. When word came that Andy and Mardy Fish were soon ready to start their doubles match, the crowd started to line up at court two. Literally, the line was five people wide and 40 deep at both entrances. The buzz was in the air and most of the crowd that was watching the Paul Goldstein-Thomas Enqvist singles match was waiting in anticipation of the doubles match to follow. In most tournaments, doubles has merely become a secondary place to hang out while waiting for the next singles to start. Doubles has ceased to be the big draw, but this afternoon it was the doubles that attracted the consciousness of the crowd. It took nearly a half-hour to seat the crowd and with each shot, applause became instantly deafening. In most Tennis games, the enthusiasm of the crowd builds to a crescendo especially with headliners. In this case, the applause began instantly, and each stroke by Roddick and Fish was greeted with howls and shrieks. Roddick and Fish put on a show and the bottom line is that very few Tennis players can command the attention that Roddick does. Sports is identified as much by individuals as their exploits. For many, Michael Jordan represented Basketball, and in earlier generations, baseball was associated with the legendary exploits of Babe Ruth. In the past, it was Jimmy Connors or John McEnroe that was the face of Men's Tennis with Pete Sampras and Andre Agassi following in their footsteps. Superstars and personality drives sports. For Tennis, the face will be Andy Roddick.

Tom and Beth Donelson, August 21, 2003

Book Design

This book has the following purposes. The first was to follow Andy's 2003 season. My daughter told me at the beginning of the year, this will be Andy's breakthrough season. So we recorded the major events of Andy's season. At the beginning of the book, we introduce the readers to the world of Tennis. With this background, the reader can see for themselves what a Tennis player must do to make a living and what it takes to put a major event together.

At the end of the book, we delve into the particulars of the game, including the art of playing doubles and the difficulty of returning a Tennis serve. The latter remains one of the most difficult aspects of the sport. We conclude with a round table discussion by three seasoned Tennis reporters on their impression of Andy Roddick's year. We invited these experts via EMAIL to answer a few questions and we simply published the unedited versions for the casual Tennis fan to observe how the Tennis World views Andy Roddick's place in Tennis.

Throughout the book, we never truly make reference to Pete Sampras as being retired until the US Open. While Sampras did not play a tournament throughout the year, he did not officially retire until the end of the year. We wrote as if he was not retired throughout the 2003 season until the very end, when he made it official.

Tom Donelson
October 5, 2003

Roddick's Parents

"We were both raised in a farm community in southwestern Wisconsin near the Iowa and Illinois border, I was the city girl and my husband was the farmer," Mrs. Roddick joked to us in an interview. The Roddicks met while in college, with Blanche Roddick becoming an English teacher after college, teaching junior high school students. On occasion she would teach French if the school was in a pinch. Jerry Roddick proved to be a successful entrepreneur, owning up to 70 Jiffy Lube franchises throughout the Midwest in Omaha and Lincoln, Nebraska, as well as in the Austin and San Antonia areas in Texas.

The Roddick's first son was an all-American diver at the University of Nebraska. Lawrence began his diving career as a young boy when he was not allowed to participate in Little League due to age, a rule that Mrs. Roddick thought preposterous since many of Lawrence's classmates participated in their neighborhood league. Mrs. Roddick suggested that Lawrence join the swim team to have something to do during the summer months. Lawrence told his mother, "I am not very good at swimming," and his mother responded, "You will learn more about swimming on the swim team than lessons." After the first day of swim team practice, Lawrence decided to switch to diving. He told his mom "divers practice at noon, it is warmer then." He first didn't like diving but as Mrs. Roddick told us, "We have a rule, if you start something, you must finish it." Eventually, Lawrence became one of America's best divers, and is, today, a successful chiropractor in San Antonio.

Their second son, John was an excellent junior Tennis player in his own right, and Mrs. Roddick commented, "John could have been at Andy's level, but had back problems that we couldn't ever get straightened out." The back problems hampered John's rise into the professional ranks though he did become an All-American at the University of Georgia. Today, John runs a Tennis club in San Antonio called Roddick Total Tennis and his wife, Ginger, is Andy's public relations person.

Their move to Texas was dictated by the warmer weather and all year Tennis. As Mrs. Roddick told us, "John, was an excellent Tennis junior and this gave John more opportunity to develop his talent." She added that many of the indoor tennis clubs in Nebraska were expensive and time on the weekend was not always available for practice. Mrs. Roddick stated that both she and her husband have always wanted to live in Austin, a love that came from Jerry's stay in San Antonio as part of his military obligation.

Mrs. Roddick joked that she was once advised to enjoy the success of their eldest since the others would not match his success. She added, "that was silly advice, so I ignored her." Mrs. Roddick said, "Our children were spaced out and they were in effect only children. So, they all got their just due…our goal was to provide and let them to be the best they can be." Mrs. Roddick told of how, when they first moved to Florida, Andy played in the 12 and under league and John was on the national team, "no one realized for eight months that Andy and John were brothers."

When asked, did she ever think that Andy would become one of the world's best Tennis players, she responded, "As a mother, I believed he was going to be very good. At his first practice when he was three and half years old, Andy hit the ball 50 consecutive times at the wall, so, we knew he had eye-hand coordination." Mrs. Roddick continued, "John McEnroe said if you know that your kid has a special talent, you develop it…. This talent should be part of his life." The Roddicks have always lived by this motto with all of their children.

Blanche Roddick said that Andy told her that autograph seekers did not bother him since he was seeking autographs himself just five years ago, and as Mrs. Roddick told us, "He is not that far removed from it." As for Andy Roddick, American sex symbol, Mrs. Roddick said, "Andy will not allow anyone to have his picture with his shirt off, and he wears his shirt in practice." Mrs. Roddick told a story of an event that occurred during the Cincinnati tournament; Brad Gilbert took off his shirt during practice, something left over from the Agassi days and while the crowd demanded the same of Andy, he kept on practicing with his shirt on.

Mrs. Roddick added a story that, after Andy completed a practice session, a young girl, who was a Down's syndrome child, gave him a hat. As he moved to the locker room, he noticed that the hat had the word down crossed out and the word Up replacing it. Andy told his mother later how touched he was by the gesture. "He can see beyond himself," Mrs. Roddick said.

Brad Gilbert is the mastermind of the psyche and keeps the practice light, so this helped relieve the pressure of being the next great thing. Mrs. Roddick stated, "You notice that during their practice, they banter with one another. This lightens the practice and relieves any pressure." Mrs. Roddick added "Pressure is part of everyday life. You can have pressure just paying your mortgage." Mrs. Roddick views the pressure on Andy as just part of the territory when you strive for excellence.

The Roddicks follow Andy on the Internet or television when they are not at the tournament, and as Mrs. Roddick joked, "When he breaks, we meet each other in the hall and give high fives when we are following him at home" Mrs. Roddick confessed a little secret that both Andy and his girlfriend, Mandy Moore, are fans of American Idol, and when it is on, they both keep up with it.

Mrs. Roddick does not consider what they have done for their children as a sacrifice as she told us, "My husband, Jerry, is a goal setter and one of his goals was to make enough money to support the boys in their athletic endeavors." For nearly ten years, Jerry worked extra hours but as Mrs. Roddick said, "We never counted the dollars." Part of the price in securing their children's futures was the extra hours of work, but then this is merely Middle America values. These are the values that produced athletic excellence; for his children have inherited their dad's work ethic. The Roddicks consider themselves a product of Middle America, and Andy is essentially the kid next door. You can say that Roddick's success began at home.

Houston Clay Court 2003

Going to a Tennis tournament is quite the event. The first couple of days of any Tennis tournament often produce upsets and drama not always seen in the later matches. For Tennis fans, it is the one time you can see all the stars. In Tennis, when a player leaves, he does not always stick around for the rest of the tournament, and Tennis is one sport in which if you lose, you're out. The only exception is the Year-end Championship or Masters Cup, which is conducted as a round robin event, with only the top eight players competing. The NCAA's tournament has gained its own popularity due to its one and out format and occasional upsets in the first weekend of play. Lose early and the bills don't get paid. Stay around to the later stages of the matches and you not only gain championship points but also can make a good living. Most tournaments feature a two out of three set format, and it is only the majors and Davis Cup that men play best three out of five. However in most tournaments, after the first rounds, a player plays everyday.

What we are talking about is that a player may have to play Tennis at a high level for six straight matches to win the title. (Seven for a major, where the player is playing the best three out of five.) The average match can last up to two hours and in majors, it could go on for three hours and longer. And certainly, there are very few sports in which athletes must have the endurance to run and perspire for two-hours—only to come back the next day and do it again. The closest sport would be professional basketball, in which players must average the equivalent of running five-seven miles hard three to four times a week—some days back to back. Even professional basketball players have a day or two to rest in between. In addition, a basketball player plays in a controlled environment in which air conditioning keeps the courts from overheating whereas a Tennis player may find himself playing in excessive heat or in substantial winds.

Professional Hockey players are similar in the exertion of exercise and you have to add the pounding that a hockey player must sustain during a game. Professional baseball players will play three or four days consecutively before moving on to the next town. However, baseball players rarely exert the same energy levels as Tennis players, with the possible exception of pitchers and catchers—the only players on the field involved in every defensive play.

The opening of the Houston Clay tournament featured a charity match sponsored by Andre Agassi. Andre Agassi has his own charity foundation, which has raised over $24 million over the past seven years, that includes opening a school for disadvantaged kids in Las Vegas, Agassi's hometown. "Las Vegas has one of the highest rates of high school drop out and teenage pregnancy," Agassi said, "This was my way to help these children finish their education." Agassi, along with Dr. Phil, discussed his charities as well as his Tennis future. Many players are involved in charities. (Andy Roddick has his own foundation, the Andy Roddick Foundation that distributes money to various causes. The foundation focuses on children and as its vision statements emphasize, the foundation will "assist, educate and rehabilitate so that no needy child will be denied their dream.")

Agassi, when asked if he missed Pete Sampras, who did not come to the Houston Clay Courts, joked, "I am not disappointed that Pete did not show up." A long time rival, these two men defined Tennis for the past decade. In one interview when asked how he still competes with the young Turks like Roddick, Agassi merely replied, "Mind and Body." Agassi said, "The reason that I can compete is mind and body. I try to better myself every day." Even when Agassi was floundering in the mid-90's, he worked on his skills and never gave up. Engaging in an extensive training program, he got himself in shape and is now playing the best of his career. Coming into Houston, Agassi was a confident player and this showed on the court and through his 18-1 record. His sense of humor was demonstrated in the charity exhibition the evening before the main tournament. With quick wit and a magical touch, Agassi and Roddick entertained the audience, often using their partners, Dr. Phil and NBA star Clyde "the glide" Dexler as props. (There were times when Dr. Phil and Dexler could hold their own both with their rackets and orally.) Early in the match, Dr. Phil wanted to test Roddick. Every chance he got he hit the ball back to Roddick, usually resulting in a losing effort. Agassi finally had enough and gave Dr. Phil the advice, "if they have hair, don't go there."

The opening weekend of any Tennis match features first of all, the qualifiers. For many qualifiers, this represents their big chance to crash the party. To fill out the remaining slots for the opening day, the qualifier must win his way into the tournament. If not, then their week is over before it begins.

One of the last qualifying matches was Jack Brasington and Cecil Mamiit. Mamiit won the first match easily 6-1. He took the first five games and appeared to be on his way to entering the main draw. Jack Brasington took the second set, 6-2 and suddenly the match turned around. As the heat took it's toll, Mamiit appeared to wilt as Jack Brasington took five of the first six games in the final set. Mamiit at one time yelled, "Courtesy please" as he could hear the faint sounds of a cell phone ringing. (The judge had to remind the audience, "turn off your cell phones.")

Mamiit dug in deep. He was determined to make one last stand, as he broke Brasington's serve. Desperation drove the match as both men proceeded to grind it down. Mamiit returned one shot literally behind his back and dove for another to save a point. Brasington just wanted to end the match then and there, but Mamiit wouldn't let the game die. Mamiit broke Brasington's serve for the first time since the first set. He easily won the next game and now it was 5-3. Brasington was still one service game up but Mamiit found his wind one more time. Brasington, at 40-40, sent one serve right pass Mamiit. Now for the final moment, Brasington unleashed his best serve yet and Mamiit returned right back in the net. After the match, Brasington headed for the player's lounge, only to be stopped. No credentials yet. The official with Brasington assured security, "yea, he just won his qualifying match, the credentials will follow." Even in victory, the reminder of what he had to go through just to get to a major event. What is the difference between the top players such as Andre Agassi and Andy Roddick and those ranked below 100? Very little but that very little seems a world apart. To the naked eye, there is very little difference in skill levels but yet the small difference, not always obvious, is seen in the results. Andre Agassi, himself has seen both sides. Beginning his career as one of America's up and coming superstars, Andre Agassi was ranked 140 in 1997. From that point on, Andre would win five more majors and began 2003 as one of the top players in the world at the age of 32. What was it about Andre, that in 1997, he was nothing but a qualifier but by 2003, he would be at the top of the Tennis world? It is as much mental as physical and Andre has stated that himself.

Players use Sunday mornings as an opportunity to practice their strokes and get used to the surface. The practice session is a play in three acts. The first act is the slow easy strokes accompanied by banters between the combatants. The second act is to practice specific shots—the lob shots, the serve, the backhand and forehand. The final act is serious practice, as each Tennis player plays hard. The final part of the drama is representative of what could happen for real.

Jeff Morrison spent his warm up with Mardy Fish as he prepared for his opening match with Andy Roddick. The easy banter gives way to serious practice but occasionally the quip comes through. As Morrison hit to Fish's backhand, Fish asked, "Are you going to use that shot tomorrow?" Morrison answers back, "going to try."

Roddick and Blake followed Morrison and Fish with their session. Roddick and Blake joked with each other as they easily strode into their practice. Roddick and then Blake practiced specific shots. First it was the backhand and then they shot at each other's forehand. All during this Tarik, Andy's coach, coached and taught. He would occasionally stride into the shot as he demonstrated what needed to be done. Roddick listened and then worked on the suggestion. Tarik watched intently throughout the entire session and acted the part of coach.

Even as the practice becomes serious, there is the occasional quip. As Roddick served up lobs to Blake and Blake hits them back. Roddick complimented Blake on his stroke, "good shot," but after one good shot and another, Blake missed his mark and smashed it out. Roddick joked, "You got greedy, James, you got greedy."

Roddick and Blake got serious and started exchanging serious hardware. Roddick occasionally showed his frustration as he missed a couple of returns. (One time, Roddick just took the ball and swatted the ball over the wall and into the next neighborhood at least 300 feet.) Roddick and Blake's competitive juices started flowing as if the final championship was on the line but after it was over, they started laughing.

There is a camaraderie that exists between players, especially the young Americans, a trait that was seen with Spanish, Australian and French players for years but not always practiced among the Americans. What made the rivalry between McEnroe and Connors so intriguing was the disdain that one shared for the other. Sampras and Agassi may have mutual respect for each other but you would never see them out socially. The current generation of American players is friendlier toward one another. After Roddick and Mardy Fish defeated Brian Vahaly and Jim Thomas in the second round doubles match, Roddick took Vahaly out to dinner at the Waffle house. James Blake had often said that his best friend on tour was Mardy Fish, who lives near Blake in Tampa. Fish even lived with Roddick and his family for a year while they both were in high school. On the court they are competitors, but off the court, a friendship exists. What exists also is an understanding that all are traveling the same path.

A couple of hours later, Roddick and Brian Vahaly practiced a few strokes. For these young players, Tennis is still a game. As the rain comes down, both players continue to play and practice. Laughing and joking, they seem to just enjoy the bantering as much as the practice strokes. As in the practice session of Jeff Morrison and Mardy Fish, they started playing for sandwiches and who would pay for lunch. Despite the high risks, there seems to be time for occasional humor or fun bets.

What does it take to run a tournament like that at Houston? Linda McIngvale, the co-owner of the Westside Tennis Club, said, "It takes an army of 170 volunteers." Linda owns the Westside Tennis Club, and along with her husband, Jim, has been instrumental in bringing professional Tennis to Houston. Linda said, "Westside is the only Tennis club in the United States that has all of the playing surfaces, clay, grass, hard court and rebound ace." Westside is the complete package so it was easy for Westside to bid for the Masters Cup, the final year-end championship of the top eight players.

In the Byzantine world of bids and negotiations, often it is whom you know, and finding the one person to fight for you. In the case of the McIngvales, it was their relationship with the Roddicks that helped sway them to go after the Masters Cup and the Davis Cup. "The Roddicks mentioned to us that we should consider going after the Masters Cup during the Davis Cup," Linda said, "I was not aware of the Masters Cup." Blanche Roddick said, "The Masters Cup used to be played in Hamburg and New York as tradition. Recently, they have been in China so we thought, why not Houston. So we discussed this with the ATP and suggested Westside Tennis Club." In a process not dissimilar to the Olympics, the McIngvales submitted a bid and a proposal and landed the Masters Cup.

The McIngvales are Houston's ambassador to Tennis. Houston Clay Court Championship has something for everyone and there is Texas written all over the tournament. A fashion show brings in the women for a one-day session, and players spend extra time to do autograph sessions, plus there is even a dunking pool for players as fans get to "dunk" favorite players. The players get a chance to play bartender at the Bacardi Bar. The McIngvales have also made it fun for players-turning what could be a chore into a contest. For every event the player is involved in, they receive points. The one with the most points wins a piece of furniture from their other business, Furniture Gallery. The key is fun for the fans and promotion of Tennis. McIngvales are Tennis fans first, and make their tournament fan friendly.

1

The Journey Begins

Part One: Roddick Down Under

Tennis season dawns under the hot Australian sun. It means a new beginning for players trying to improve on last year while bringing a challenge to others to keep their current form. Some took time off to relax and go on vacation after a long season, some tried to recover from the nagging injuries that plagued them all of last year, but at one time or another they all went back to work and trained for the first slam of the year. The Australian Open. The first major.

Traditionally, the Aussie Open, as it has become known, starts in the third week of January. Just before the New Year the ATP (Association of Tennis Professionals) swarms into Chennai, Doha and Adelaide. Those who are not early risers wait a week to go to either Auckland or Sydney. Players have two weeks of potential warm-up time before the main event in Melbourne.

Among those players who choose the Adidas International Open in Sydney is Andy Roddick. Since he burst on the tennis scene in early 2001, he had been touted as "the future of American Tennis" and the "most likely to succeed Pete Sampras and Andre Agassi." A tall task for anyone, considering the two combine for 22 Grand Slam titles and counting. Roddick at age 20, in his two full years on the tour hasn't been able to live up to the expectations of some. A good-looking kid with an attractive game makes him a target for advertisers. He has often been good for a sound bite for the media, and his game perfect for Sport Center highlights has made him a fan favorite around the world, and vulnerable. His sophomore year brought mixed success. He ended the 2002 season ranked number 10 in the world, a 54-22 record and two titles, but fell short of a breakthrough in a major. He wasn't able to improve on any of his previous Grand Slam Performances. He came into the 2003 Australian Open not getting past the third round other than at the US Open. He had been to the quarterfinals of the previous two US Opens, both times losing to the eventual champions.

But that was 2002 and in the past. Roddick had spent most of November and all of December gearing up for his 2003 campaign. He spent hours working on his fitness, and correcting his weaknesses-his backhand and net game. He had one goal in mind-to make it to the Masters Cup in Houston and all else would fall into place. To make it to the Masters Cup in Houston later that year meant that Roddick had to hit the upper elite ranks of Tennis. The Australian Open would be the first test for the 2003 season though he would start at the Adidas International Tournament in Sydney. This would be his warm-up for the Aussie Open.

In Sydney, Roddick would meet another 20 year old, Tommy Robredo, in the first round. When they first met in the round of 16 at the 2001 US Open, it was thought that they would both be future champions, though Robredo had yet to make the same leap as Roddick. Robredo was still hanging around the top 30 and has made several appearances in the top 20, but had yet to win a set off Roddick. This day in Sydney was no different. Roddick quickly dispatched Robredo 6-2, 6-2 on that Tuesday night to start off his season and was relieved to finally get back on the court. His second round match though would be no walk in the park.

Hyung-Taik Lee of Korea was a veteran of the tour and hard worker but had yet to win a tour title. Lee and Roddick have played five times before, all going Roddick's way though they were tough matches. In 2002, they played in Sydney in the quarterfinals. Roddick was close to losing that match. He was down a break in the third set before storming back to a 7-5 victory. On this day, Roddick and Lee, had their usual tight match but also had the elements to deal with. Sydney was going through a pretty ferocious windstorm with winds up to 60 mph. Any tennis player will tell you that out of all the conditions one could play in, wind is the least desirable. It wrecks havoc on the ball toss of their serves and makes it even harder to place groundstrokes. A big server like Roddick who depended on his serve to get him out of trouble was having trouble with the conditions. In the end the weather and Lee was too much for Roddick and he lost 7-6, 7-5. Cutting his warm-up to the Australian Open short.

Heading to Melbourne early after a disappointing loss, a still optimistic Roddick believed that he had a good chance of winning. He had spent most of the off-season working on his fitness and was eager to prove it.

In his first round against Krajan (Zeijko), Andy lost the first set in the tiebreak after being up 4 to 1 in the set. The Australian Open has always had a history of upset surprises and already, former champion Jennifer Capriati was eliminated in the first round on the women's side. Losing the first set was not a good omen for Roddick. It was important for Roddick to get through this first match and a lot was riding on his performance here. Many critics were harping on Andy's lack of success at the slams outside the US Open. After the loss of the first set he recovered to take the second set easily but in the third, he lost a service break early. He managed to win the third set in a tiebreaker. Up two sets to one, Roddick was struggling to find his game against an overmatched opponent until the fourth set when Roddick put his game together, winning easily 6-3.

There really isn't much to say about Roddick's second and third round matches. After his first round scare, he easily dispatched Adrian Voinea, in three straight 6-2 sets in the second round and Fernando Vicente 6-2, 6-3, 6-2 in the third. Now, Andy faced a rival that he had yet to beat. Mikhail Youzhny, like Roddick, was an up and coming star. At the age of 20, this young talent was part of a young contingent of new stars that included Marat Safin coming out of Russia. And in two previous matches, Youzhny had defeated Roddick in straight sets. Roddick had not only lost to Youzhny but hadn't even managed to take a set from him. Youzhny had white washed the young American, and appeared to have his number. So far!!

Youzhny stood between Roddick and the quarterfinals, and a possible date with Lleyton Hewitt, and Roddick stood between Youzhny and his first quarterfinals. Hewitt was getting ready to play Moroccan Younes El Aynaoui at Rod Laver Arena, the main stadium court, while Roddick and Youzhny were battling it out next door at Vodafone Arena. For Roddick, the pressure was building. With James Blake and Mardy Fish both eliminated, Roddick was the lone remaining player of the new lions of American Tennis. The only other American still playing was the ageless Andre Agassi. The first test of the 2003 season was to begin. Youzhny was seeded 25th but as far as Roddick was concerned, he might as well be listed number one. Against Roddick, Youzhny played as if he was the best in the world.

Youzhny took the first set in a tiebreaker and easily took the second set earning himself an early break in the third set, probably thinking at that point he would have another easy victory over Roddick. At this point, Roddick showed his guts. Roddick admitted that in the past, he would not have been able to make such a comeback. "Between the ears, I probably would have gotten too frustrated. It might have overwhelmed me. Physically, I don't know if I could have gotten through it either," he told the press after the match. All the training he worked on in November and December was about to pay off. Down 4 games to one in the crucial third set and facing elimination, Roddick came back to win six out of the next seven games to take the set.

After being outplayed and out hustled, Roddick found new resolve, and when he won the third set, one mental block had been removed. Roddick finally won his first set against Youzhny. Though down two sets to one, Roddick eliminated his first mental hurdle, knowing he could beat his Russian rival. With the serve clicking and his game humming, he took the last two sets in easy fashion, 6-3, 6-2.

Roddick commented after the match, "Some days it just does, I guess. You know, it was in his hands. He kind of gave me a break back, played his first bad game of the match in the third set. I played a really strong game to win the third set. From then on I was feeling, 'It's anybody's match,'" It was more than just a victory against an opponent he'd never beaten but was also the first time he came back from two sets to love and win.

Andy's conclusion about this match was, "I made strides in each of those and it showed during this tourney. The match against Youzhny was a big step for me. I would have normally gotten frustrated being two sets down and feeling like nothing was working. For the first time in my career, I stayed calm in that situation and then proceeded to play some of my best tennis from there on out."

When asked by one reporter if this match would prove to be a turning point, Roddick merely stated, "It's good. It keeps me alive for another round, which is the goal going into the day. (It) just happened in a more dramatic fashion than any other days." Roddick's thoughts turned to Lleyton Hewitt. Hewitt and Roddick staged a dramatic five set clash in the 2001 US Open in the quarterfinals. It was this match that propelled Hewitt to the top and to his first Grand Slam victory over Pete Sampras. Soon, Roddick, like the rest of the Tennis world, would be shocked at the new development. Younes El Aynaoui upset Hewitt in a tough four-setter. The rematch between Hewitt and Roddick would have to wait another day. Roddick was about to engage in one of the greatest Tennis matches of all times.

Going into his match with Younes El Aynaoui, the pressure started to mount on Roddick. This was his third Grand Slam quarterfinal and now it was time to take the next step. With Hewitt out, Roddick was the heavy favorite to reach the semifinals. El Aynaoui played the match of his life as he defeated the number one player in the world Hewitt, two nights before. Roddick exorcised some demons of his own as he finally beat the Russian Mikhail Youzhny. For Roddick, his victory over Youzhny was more than personal redemption, for as America's future hope in Tennis, Roddick had to bear the crush of potential not yet realized on his shoulders. For Roddick's critics, nothing short of an Australian final would do. And everyone was talking of a possible Roddick-Agassi final.

El Aynaoui had already played the match of his life and rarely are there two such matches in one tournament for a player of El Aynaoui's stature. El Aynaoui took the first game, breaking Roddick's serve and thus serving notice that indeed, he might yet have one more miracle in his hip pocket. Roddick took the second set by a tiebreaker and the match was on. The third set ended in controversy as a good Roddick return was called out; thus giving the set to El Aynaoui. Nip and tuck, both men's serve prove to be decisive factors as they rarely broke each other. Spectacular shot followed spectacular shot and Roddick tied the match up by keeping his nerve and winning the fourth set. All game long, both men played superb Tennis, and this was not a case of one man losing to another but of both men refusing to submit to the other's will. Hardly ever in sports do you see two men playing at such a high level with so few mistakes in the same match?

What make's this match memorable was the ending. Like the other majors with the exception of the U.S. Open, the fifth set can't be settled by a tiebreaker. So for the next two and a half hours, both men pounded each other, never surrendering. In one dramatic moment in the 10th game of the fifth set, Roddick saved one match point with a fantastic inside-out forehand that painted the line. This was a statement by Roddick that if he were going to lose, it would be with his best shot. Roddick broke serve in the 21st game as he took an 11-10 lead and now he had service. Roddick appeared on the verge of victory but El Aynaoui was not ready to have the match end there. He broke Roddick's serve and the match was tied again. After the 38th game, the match appeared no closer to conclusion than at the beginning of the match. The players, exhausted, took a break and Roddick, the showman that he was, gave his racket to a ball boy to return El Aynaoui shots as he went to sit down. El Aynaoui, not to be outdone, gave his racket to another ball boy to serve. To the delight of the fans, the two ball boys played a point and the players received their breather. But shortly it was back to business and despite fatigue settling in, both players maintained the highest levels of Tennis. There was no erosion of skills, as both men did not allow fatigue to affect the quality of their play. You got the impression that both men could have gone another 38 games.

Roddick finally broke Aynaoui's serve to take a 20-19 lead and now he had to hold serve. Roddick put in one big effort to end the match. Roddick rushed to a 40-0 lead. On the first match point, Roddick lunged for a volley, hitting it just wide. Almost in shock that the match wasn't over, he went back to serve the last point. The last point came as both men exchanged shots. Roddick hit to Aynaoui back—hand, and Aynaoui's return smashed into the net, finally ending this classic match.

This match was similar to a boxing match with both men absorbing the best that each other had. After the game, both men realized that they were part of something special as they shook each other's hand in congratulatory fashion. Roddick felt humbled by victory and was now in a semifinal of a major for the first time. El Aynaoui reached his own personal heights. At the age of 31, El Aynaoui has toiled at the periphery of the upper reaches of the Tennis world. A good player, El Aynaoui was not a top ten performer. For two matches, he played like one—realizing that at 31, there were very few more chances at a major. Roddick's victory over El Aynaoui took Roddick to new levels. With these two victories over El Aynaoui and Youzhny, Roddick appeared in his first major semifinal.

Andy reflected after the match, "And then came the match with El Aynaoui… still not sure what to really say about it other than it was an honor to take part in such a well-played match. I couldn't believe we played for that long. But the thing I really couldn't believe was the stats when I looked at them after the match. It was truly a special match and I am not sure if I will ever play in another like it."

What stood between his first final and a date with Andre Agassi was the German Rainer Schuettler. As the 31st seed, Schuettler was appearing in his first semi finals. At the age of 26, Schuettler was now the surprise entry in the final four. Roddick, just like against El Aynaoui, was the heavy favorite and most Americans and commentators were already penciling a Roddick-Agassi final.

Unbeknownst to tennis fans, Roddick severely injured his wrist during a fifth-set fall, lunging for the volley on the first match point against El Aynaoui and this injury would sideline Roddick for several weeks after the tournament. Ailing and still exhausted from his classic match against El Aynaoui, Roddick lost the first set 7-5.

Roddick easily took the second set and all appeared well. The Agassi-Roddick final match emerged on the horizon. Then the exhaustion and injured wrist played into the match. Denied his powerful serve, unable to really hold a racket and in pain, Roddick could no longer compete against the German. After the match, Roddick admitted, "I knew going out there it was sore…but it didn't get better." Roddick's own thought was that the wrist would get better as the match continued and the adrenaline started pumping. It did not, but then Roddick was not going to quit either. Once before, he withdrew from a major, the 2001 French Open, as well as last year's Australian Open, and was determined it was not going to happen again. After losing the first set, he bound a white strapping around a blue sweatband to cushion the blows. He managed to take the second round but finally surrendered to the inevitable. The wrist could not hold out and Schuettler took the last two sets to win the match. In the last set, Roddick tripped and fell over a plant box at the edge of the court, where he'd picked up an Elmo doll that fell out of the stand. Schuettler told the gathering press after the match, "Right now I'm really speechless." Schuettler reached a major final for the first time.

Afterward, Roddick did not use his injured wrist or his conditioning coming after the El Aynaoui match as an excuse. When asked about his defeat, Roddick commented, "He won the big points when he had to…he played a smart match. All credit, he deserves to be in the final."

The Australian Open would be remembered for two major events. Serena Williams winning her fourth major in a row, beating big sister Venus, and Andre Agassi winning his eighth major in easy fashion.

For Roddick, this grand slam was a success. He reached the semifinals for the first time in a major; he defeated Mikhail Youzhny and served notice that he was ready to compete with the elite players. 2003 got off to a rousing success.

Roddick wrote in his diary after the Open, "The three things that I really wanted to work on in the off season were fitness, aggressiveness (coming to the net, taking my chances, etc.), and keeping my head on my shoulders. I felt that I made strides in each of those and it showed during this tourney."

Part Two: The Davis Cup

One of Andy's biggest disappointments was missing the US Davis Cup against Croatia and the American Davis Cup team missed Roddick. The Croatians had the home field advantage with a fast court that benefited their big servers. Roddick's big serve and a Davis Cup experience would have helped the undermanned and inexperienced Americans. With Roddick out with his wrist injury, and Agassi and Sampras having put their Davis Cup days behind them; James Blake was pushed into the number one slot that had been reserved for Andy Roddick.

One of Patrick McEnroe's first moves as the new Davis Cup Captain in 2001 was to recruit an inexperienced 18-year-old Andy Roddick. Speaking with Roddick's coach, Tarik Benhabiles, McEnroe asked if Andy was available to play Davis Cup. At this time, Roddick was ranked outside the top 100 and playing a challenger tournament in Hawaii. With a victory in Hawaii, over another up and comer at the time James Blake, the young teenager showed up for his first Davis Cup against Switzerland. Upon arrival, Roddick's firepower impressed the coach and veteran Todd Martin. McEnroe recalled, "When Todd saw his firepower, we just looked at each other and shook our heads." Roddick took his first Davis Cup singles match, a close battle with Swiss George Bastl. Unfortunately, the match did not impact the final result. The US was eliminated by Switzerland, three matches to two. Roddick would go on to win his next six straight Davis Cup singles before losing in Paris in September of 2002.

Over the years, a rapport has developed between McEnroe and Roddick. For McEnroe, his respect for Roddick's natural talent is unlimited. For Roddick, he is forever indebted to McEnroe's faith in his talent and allowing him an early opportunity to participate in the Davis Cup. For McEnroe, there is a fine line between being a mentor and a coach. Tennis players have their own coaches and Roddick's coach is Brad Gilbert. As McEnroe stated, "I'm not a coach and there's no confusion about that." McEnroe represents an extra eye, and for Roddick a relationship has developed between the young Tennis star and the Davis Cup captain.

The relations were strained between McEnroe and the players' coaches during the Switzerland—United States Davis Cup match when McEnroe closed practice to the players' coaches. McEnroe's reason was that he did not want too many coaches in the kitchen, as he would later quip. McEnroe, ever aware of diplomacy, consulted privately with his players and their coaches. This was important, as he was aware as a former player himself that jealousy could develop between coaches and the Davis Cup Captain.

When the younger McEnroe took over for his older and more accomplished brother, John McEnroe, he brought with him a new attitude to the Davis Cup. He wanted to bring the new generation of American players on to the team. Patrick not only brought in a young Roddick for his first time, he added Blake as his second singles player to play against India in September 2001. Constantly asked why not recruit either Sampras or Agassi, McEnroe always responded that he only wanted players that desired to be there, and that he had found them in the young guys. He tried to make it a team affair as the players stayed in the same hotel, ate dinner together and he made sure there was a ping-pong table for the guys to play with. The camaraderie that McEnroe created not only with Andy and James, but Mardy Fish, Robby Ginepri and Taylor Dent brought the young Americans closer as a team and, more importantly, focused as a group to win the Davis Cup for the US.

During the week of September 16, before last years France—United States semi-final tie, McEnroe worked on Andy Roddick's ability to move in on the ball. McEnroe barked out orders and on occasion, Andy would rebel. As McEnroe stated later, "One of the joys of working with Andy is that he lets you know how he feels."

Unfortunately for the U.S., the French on their home clay surface, proved too tough for the young and improving American team. Roddick was disappointed with the result as he lost back-to-back matches to Arnaud Clement and Sebastian Grosjean. This match, however, moved Roddick's skills forward. The disappointment in Paris, only made missing Croatia even more painful for Roddick because he was unable to play for his country and help them win.

For Roddick, the Croatian match represented his chance for redemption from his performance against the French and was an important step forward. Without Roddick, the American team proved unable to compete. Even the Croatians acknowledged that without Roddick, the Americans were at a disadvantage.

James Blake was an excellent choice to replace Andy as the number one player. Having worn a back brace for 18 hours a day as a teenager to correct severe scoliosis, James Blake demonstrated his own skills and courage in the world of Tennis. Blake showed his mettle on the first day of the Davis Cup as he evened the match by beating Mario Ancic but without Roddick; Blake was alone in carrying the American staff. The good news was that like Roddick, Blake had a good record in Davis Cup having only lost one singles match.

Mardy Fish opened the match by losing to Ivan Ljubicic in the first match. A Davis Cup competition centered on the doubles match and this event was not any different. The American team of Fish and Blake took on Ljubicic and Goran Ivanisevic. Blake was undefeated in Davis Cup doubles matches. With Goran suffering from a shoulder injury that kept him out of most of last season, the Americans were favored to take the doubles. The week before Goran pulled out of a challenger event in Germany because of it and, with questions still remaining about his fitness, the Americans appeared to have the advantage. The first two sets went the Americans way, but the veteran Ivanisevic and Ljubicic took the third set to a tiebreaker. A 7-4 tiebreaker score turned the tide, and the two Croatians took control and swept the next two sets.

The next morning Blake lost only his second Davis Cup singles match to Ljubicic, and the Americans were eliminated from competition for this year. Davis Cup is one tournament where home turf matters. When the French or the Spanish choose the clay surfaces, this fits their players' styles and minimizes those countries whose strength is power. In Croatia, the surface was a fast indoor carpet and was built to accentuate the power game of the Croatians. Ljubicic, Ivanisevic and the young Ancic were big slammers, and without Roddick, the Americans were missing the one player whose strength and skills was perfect for this court. However disappointing that the Americans' performance was, this proved to be a learning experience as Fish and Blake learned how to play on the grand stage. For these young players, the Davis Cup is the one event that prepares them mentally for the majors. It is at the majors where a Tennis player's fame is made. For the young Americans like Fish, Blake and Roddick, the Davis Cup was the perfect training ground for the big tournaments as they learned to play pressure Tennis against some of the world's best.

Andy's own thought after the Davis Cup was, "The biggest disappointment came a couple days later when I found out I wasn't going to be able to play for my country in the first round Davis Cup tie against Croatia. The boys went over there and gave it their all and I am extremely proud to call them my friends. I can't wait to get back on court with them next time."

Part Three: Kroger St. Jude Open

After almost a month away from the tour, it was comeback time for Andy as he prepared to test his sore wrist. Without pain and showing only a few signs of rust, Roddick began defending his title at the Kroger St. Jude Tournament in Memphis, with an opening thrashing of Cecil Mamiit 6-4, 6-4. Roddick stated that he felt good and complained only of stiffness from not playing over the previous two weeks. With James Blake and Paradorn Srichaphan winning their first matches rather easily, Roddick put himself on target to defend his championship. Roddick delivered his one-two punch of a ferocious first-serve and whipping inside-out forehand and the rust melted away as the match proceeded. Roddick explained his strategy, "I've become better at the net. I've got a 135 mph serve, so I'd be stupid not to follow that in. Overall I'm a better player than I was last year."

The second round proved a tougher match. Despite having beaten Lee five out of the six previous matches, he did lose his previous contest in Australia in a wind filled match. As he marched into the quarterfinals, or maybe more accurately, limped into the quarterfinals, he was the only seeded player left. Both James Blake and Paradorn Srichaphan were eliminated in upsets. American Mardy Fish took care of the second seed Paradorn Srichaphan and Blake lost to Georgian Irakli "The Freak" Labadze, who had yet to win an ATP match this year, and lost in the first round of eight of the previous nine ATP tournament events.

Roddick was the last match of the night and Hyung-Taik Lee opened up by beating Roddick in the first set. "The people who stay there to the end are the die hards," Roddick said, "They really pulled me through this one."

Roddick did not break Lee until the 10th game of the second set, and leveled the match at one set apiece. The final match was a nip and tuck affair. In the 10 games of the deciding set, Lee took a 15-40 lead on Roddick's serve. Threatening to break serve and end the set, Lee had to deal with Roddick's newfound maturity and grittiness. Roddick rallied and hit a forehand winner that sent the audience into a tizzy. Roddick's holding serve in the 10th game had the crowd on its feet and Roddick's spirits soared. Lee had yet one more chance to break Roddick's serve and end the match; and one more time Roddick dipped into the well and preserved his serve.

The match was now to be decided in a tiebreaker. Roddick earned a mini break and opened up with a 3-zip lead as he nailed a 133 mph serve to hit the third point. Prevailing in the tiebreaker, Roddick now prepared for the quarterfinal match against fellow American Ginepri.

"I had a bit of luck and played some clutch points in the third," an elated Roddick said after the match. "I stayed in it. I'm still not feeling at my best from the baseline and I'm lucky to have a serve that can keep me in matches." Roddick's experience in Australia made him a tougher player and now he realized that he can comeback from any situation.

The Roddick and Ginepri friendship goes back to the juniors when they were 11 years old. Since their junior days, they have stayed good friends even though after all these years, Ginepri had yet to beat Roddick. Roddick did have his fears for this match though, for Ginepri had the tools to pull off the upset, and so far, the only consistent thing in this tournament was that seeded players were heading home early. Roddick and Ginepri held serve until Roddick broke his serve in the ninth game in the first set.

Roddick served 13 aces and with service break in the ninth game, the game turned in Roddick's favor. Ginepri was unable to break through Roddick's serve and found he would be forced to play the perfect game. And perfect games hard to obtain. Roddick broke serve in the second set and this pretty much ended it all. He closed out the match in 1 hour and 10 minutes—a shorter match than the previous match against Hyung-Taik Lee. Roddick told reporters after this match, "He played a good match but I managed to serve out the big points." Roddick did not feel comfortable in the match but it did not stop him from dominating. Roddick demonstrated a champion heart. Champions win even when all the pieces are not there. Another sign of the maturity of his game.

With four Americans reaching the semifinals, Roddick joked, "I bet an American is going to win." One of the semifinal matches featured Andy Roddick and fellow countryman Brian Vahaly. Roddick won the first set 7-5 and then blitzed Vahaly in the second set. Roddick was now in the finals for the second year in a row. In the second set, he did not even lose a point on his service. Roddick was happy to be in the finals after playing probably his best game. "I didn't expect to be in the finals after taking four weeks off, but you just find ways to win," Roddick said after the match. Roddick was playing pain free and now faced Taylor Dent in the finals.

Vahaly was suffering from the flu and so was not at his best. It is tough enough to play Roddick healthy, but not being 100% added to his disadvantage. After a competitive first set, Vahaly was feeling the effects of dehydration and could no longer maintain the level of the first set. After the match, Vahaly rushed into the locker room. Vahaly admitted that Roddick "dictated play with his serve." Vahaly attempted to stall his sickness with Pepsi and Tylenol. He inhaled sugar and sugar containing products for energy. But Roddick's serve and Vahaly illness combined to force an early night on Vahaly.

Interestingly enough, Vahaly apologized to the fans for not being in shape to sign autographs after the match. Vahaly was throwing up in the locker room, but after the match was happy that he was in his first ATP semifinal. Tennis players do have a special relationship with their fans and they are more accessible to their fans than in other sports. Autographs are no longer an automatic part of other sports and more often than not; autographs are granted for a fee. In Tennis, it is different. After the game, win or lose, Tennis players usually will sign autographs for fans as they leave the court. Vahaly, like other Tennis players, felt an obligation to the fans. For a Tennis player, it is the fans that support their salaries. Unless you are a big star, there are no advertisement dollars. There are no major television revenues to support tennis. This can be contrasted to football, which is heavily subsidized by the major networks and ESPN. The players make their money by winning and advancing in the tournament. Vahaly's comments showed the relationship between Tennis players and their fans.

Roddick was the heavy favorite to win the final but Taylor Dent had his own plans. Dent, whose last ATP title was the Newport title a year ago, swept Roddick in this final. In 2002, Dent upset Blake and in the process, made history by making him and his father the first parent and son to both have ATP titles in the open era. This final was another step forward for Dent, who was beating a top ten player.

Dent dominated the first set easily, breaking Roddick's serve in the fourth and the sixth game of the first set. He took the first set 6-1. Roddick also lost his service game in the eight game of the second set. Unable to break Dent's own service game, Roddick was doomed. He had one chance to break Dent's serve at 4-3. Roddick took advantage of a Dent double fault and some good returns to get a 0-40 lead, but Dent held on and won the next five points. He lost the second set 6-4. Dent was hot, having won 24 consecutive service games without being broken.

He carried his previous momentum over from the last tournament and Roddick played the game flatfooted.

Dent credited his fitness work with his coach as a major factor. "My movement around the court has been 10 times better than it has been in the past," Dent said, "We've been doing cardio work on the bike, which was an absolute nightmare." Dent's reward for his victory was a day off and a pizza. Dent had everything on it "except anchovies," joked Dent.

Roddick was appearing in his eighth career final and played well after recovering from his wrist injuries. On this day, Roddick ran into a buzz saw—a player at his best. As Roddick noted, "I hit a second serve at 129 mph, he chipped and charged off it." Dent was not quite a top 20 player but as Roddick noted, Dent's time could be coming.

For American Tennis fans and critics, this tournament proved that American Tennis might just be alive and kicking. Americans provided six of the eight quarterfinals and an All—American final. For Roddick, the second place finish showed that he was back and ready to compete with the elites.

Part Four: Andy at Delray Beach And Indian Wells

Andy Roddick, coming off an impressive performance at the St. Jude Kroger Open in Memphis, was the number one seed in the International Tennis Championship in Delray Beach, Florida. Roddick considered Delray his hometown tournament. It's just a few miles away from his home in Boca Raton, and it allows him to sleep in his own bed at night. Another plus was that his friends and family could come out and see him. Roddick, the heavy favorite, appeared ready to play as he opened his tournament play with a doubles victory alongside his partner Brian Vahaly. Roddick and Vahaly defeated the team of Cermak and Friedl, 5-7, 7-6 (7-1 in the tie breaker) and 6-2.

Roddick in his first round match was paired against Mardy Fish. Fish, like Roddick, was part of a new generation of American Tennis players. 21 years of age, Fish practiced frequently with Roddick, a personal friend. Both men knew each other well, which made it a tough match for Roddick. Not only was he playing a friend but one who worked out with him on a routine basis. One who knew his strengths and weaknesses. There would be no surprises between these two.

Roddick started off hot, wining 5 of the first 7 games. In the eighth game Roddick was ready to finish out the first set, as he had Fish down 40-love on Fish's serve. Fish came back to take the game and then the next four out of five games. Roddick could not finish Fish, and Fish took 7 out of 11 points in the tiebreaker. For Fish as well as Roddick, Delray was his back yard.

The second set stayed on serve, and with Fish ahead 4-3, Roddick took a spill. After Roddick fell, he immediately grabbed his ankle and was unable to finish. The anguish in his eyes said it all. He could no longer compete and would have to leave the third tournament in his career due to an injury. His previous time was the Australian Open with a wrist injury. Roddick would say later, "I'm disappointed because physically I felt fine. I could've gone for hours." But Roddick was unable to continue, unable to run on the ankle. Fish was as disappointed. Fish told reporters after the match, "I can't think of a worse way to win, especially when you're playing a friend." Fish was happy with his play at that point but, "You're trying to beat him but when that happens, you want to know he's okay." For Fish, this victory was tainted for he wanted to beat his good friend on the court, not through injuries.

Fish had already beaten Carlos Moya twice in January during the Australian hard court swing but this victory was even bigger for he was beating one of the top six tennis players in the world. The opening pairings featured many upsets. Michel Krotochvil defeated number fifth seed Arnaud Clement and Sargis Sargsian upset the number two seed, Guillermo Coria. And number 7th seed Stefan Koubek took an early plane ride home as he lost to qualifier Robert Kenderick.

The biggest surprise was Fish taking out Roddick, and Roddick's sprained ankle. For Roddick, this was the second major injury in this tennis season that threatened to sideline him for an extended period of time. Early in the year, he lost nearly one month due to a sprained wrist and now was limping on a sprained ankle with Indian Wells coming up. There was no telling how long he would be out. For Roddick this was the time to start gearing up for the French Open and Wimbledon. Now his ankle sprain threatened to delay his preparation for these two majors.

As for Fish, this was his first match against Roddick since their junior days. As Fish commented, "We know each others game well…I'm use to hitting with him and we practice a lot together." The only other time that these two individuals actually competed was in the juniors when Fish was 15 and Roddick 14. Fish's recollection of that match was that it was close. "He beat me 7-6, 7-6."

Fish quipped that he had to scrounge up 30 tickets for family and friend. Fish stated, "I knew we would play each other sooner or later." For Fish, it was ironic that both men would essentially play in their back yard not far for where they practiced with each other. For Fish, it was bittersweet, for while he defeated Roddick, Roddick lost due to an injury. For Roddick, the injury bug that had beset him since the Australian Open was coming back to haunt him.

Roddick recovered quickly as he prepared for Indian Wells. While it was feared that the ankle injury could sideline Andy for up to a month, the injury turned out less severe than originally suspected. He was ready for Indian Wells. Upon his arrival the courts were a buzz with the withdrawal of Andre Agassi due to a shoulder injury. Roddick saw his draw open a little bit because Agassi pulled out. The favorite, Lleyton Hewitt the defending champion, drew the talented Younes El Aynaoui in his first round opener. The last time these two met was in round 16 at the Australian Open, a near perfect El Aynaoui upset Hewitt. The table was being set for Roddick to make a good run in his first appearance at Indian Wells.

Susan Seemiller, a tennis writer, visited with Andy before the first match. Seemiller, who had met Roddick on previous occasions, most notably after the US's defeat of France in the Davis Cup in Paris the year before, asked how the ankle was and Roddick replied, "It was doing very well actually." Seemiller saw a few of Andy's workouts at Indian Wells and felt that Roddick was moving well. Tarik Benhabiles made the decision the Friday before Indian Wells that Andy was ready after a hopeful workout.

Andy went into Indian Wells with his number sixth ranking and an impressive 10-3 record. His opponent was the Swedish player Thomas Enqvist, who had won 19 titles, a former top 10 player and a penchant for upsets. The last time these two met was in Stuttgart where Enqvist prevailed in a tight match 6-3, 6-7, 7-6.

A reporter once stated that Roddick played Tennis as if it was a contact sport resembling his favorite college football team, the Nebraska Cornhuskers. Against Enqvist, Roddick let loose his monster serve and Enqvist was back peddling the entire night. One monster serve after another, Roddick's balls were streaking past the 130 mph mark. In the second set, one of his serves approached 150 mph and the Swede was not able to break Andy's serve.

Roddick, after spending the previous week recovering from his ankle injury, seemed to move freely and not be affected by the injury. Moving along the baseline and returning Enqvist's serve or volleys, Roddick looked relaxed and as Susan Seemiller reported, "Andy played well, and served very well...Enqvist had a few opportunities but Andy did not give him much room". She also observed that Roddick "appeared to have a distressing golf ball shaped lump on his ankle. Not sure what is up with that, but he said, (in his post match interview) it was his ligament doing something funky." Andy appeared to be limping after the match, but knowing that the press would ask about his ankle, Roddick decided to play a little joke on them by putting a golf ball in his sock. Next up was Spanish up and comer Feliciano Lopez. According to Patrick McEnroe, Lopez was a big banger with a wicked forehand. For Roddick, this match was no gimme.

When asked about his ankle, Andy remarked, "It's a little swollen (laughter). We're going to try to get that down tonight (pointing to a golf ball stuck inside his sock). I'm okay to play tomorrow. I think that's one of my tendons or a couple rolled up (laughter). It's killing me." "I think I did a decent job of that all night. It's tough to play aggressive all the time against a guy like Thomas, who is pretty much cranking out on every shot," Andy said, "You have to mix it up and pick your spots. I think I did a pretty decent job of that tonight."

Andy, after the match stated about Lopez, "I've never played him. I've never practiced with him. Big lefty, big serve, pretty big forehand. You can pretty much count on the Spanish guys having pretty good feel around the court. He's been coming along in the last year or so."

Andy Roddick continued using his booming serves as he defeated Lopez 6-4, 6-3 in his second round victory. Roddick's domination was seen as he won 24 of his 28 points on first serves and had seven aces against the young Spaniard to follow up the 15 aces the night before. Roddick said after the match that the serve was the best part of his game against Lopez, and added that his serve was, "something I can normally count on. Outside of that, I feel like I played pretty well."

After the match, Roddick, responding to questions about his ankle, said, "Yeah, I feel all right. It was a good test for me. Now I have the rest of the afternoon to take care of what needs to be taken care of. I'll be ready to go tomorrow."

There are times when an athlete is not playing up to his potential or is facing another player who is at his best. Roddick had that opponent in Sebastien Grosjean. Grosjean and Roddick both live in Boca Raton together and practice with each other every so often. Friends on and off the court, Grosjean has appeared twice at Roddick's charity event. The last time they played was on the clay courts of Roland Garros, when France defeated the US in Davis Cup. It went to four sets but Roddick was no match for Grosjean and the French fans, even though he had major support from over 500 US fans. Grosjean and Roddick faced each on center court as the premier match of the night on ESPN TV. Roddick's serve in the first set was as powerful as it has been in all of his tournaments. Unfortunately, Grosjean was returning Roddick's 130 mph plus serves. Roddick's game plan was attacking every short ball after bombing his opponent with his fast serves and fearsome forehands. Grosjean and Roddick held serve and the first set was decided by a tiebreaker, 7-5 with Roddick prevailing.

Grosjean favored his forehand and his serve was a sneaky-fast serve. With the experience of being on clay, Grosjean had the patience to go toe-to-toe with Roddick and enough power to compete with the younger American.

Grosjean dominated the second set 6-2. Roddick was broken twice. Grosjean, using a vast array of shots, had Roddick on his head. Going into the final set,

Grosjean had the momentum in his favor and now it was up to Roddick to dig in and turn an apparent defeat into victory. Grosjean matched Roddick serve for serve. The final set was similar to the first. Roddick defended his serve as did Grosjean. Both men had the audience gasping with each shot and every point had game breaker written on it. Neither man could dominate the other and once again, it came to a tiebreaker. Roddick lost the first point on his serve and now Grosjean had the advantage. Roddick scored the next five points as he broke through Grosjean's serve. With the score 6-1, Roddick was in the driver's seat for the first time in the match. He finished the night with a nasty serve and volley. The tiebreaker was the only time during the match that Roddick looked in command. Throughout the entire night, Grosjean held his serve, and forced Roddick to play the perfect game in the last set. "He just came up with the goods. Second and third set, I really wasn't in my groove," Roddick said, "He played well. He served pretty well, high percentage." When asked about Grosjean's ability to return his serve, Roddick told reporters, "Well, Sebastien has great hands. You know, he's quick enough to kind of react. Those are two things. I thought he was doing a great job of putting them high and deep, giving himself a chance to get back in the court." So despite winning fewer games in the match, Roddick still came out the winner.

Roddick's ankle appeared to be feeling better, and he was surprised about his progress. He said, "I didn't play much coming into the tournament. I'm surprised, to be honest. I didn't know how far I was going to get. If you would have told me quarters before the week started, I would have been pretty happy with that." During the Tiebreaker, Roddick took the advice given to him by Pete Sampras by trying to be "most aggressive person in the tiebreaker." Roddick added, ". If I lose it, that's fine, because I was the one trying to make things happen." Roddick admitted that he was not in the grove in either the second or third set but prevailed by sheer guts. With Grosjean at the top of his game, Roddick hung in the game and in the final tiebreaker put his game together. Now he was to play Ranier Schuettler in a rematch of their semifinal match in the Australia Open.

Schuettler had made a habit of running into Roddick when Andy was injured and had a long match the night before. This time Roddick was still fatigued from his match with Grosjean and was now dealing with a sore knee in addition to his sore ankle. Roddick came out with his knee wrapped from all the extra stress he had put on it, to compensate from putting too much stress on his ankle. The run at Indian Wells ended. Roddick's movement was hampered and for the second time a compromised Roddick could not match the German Ranier Schuettler as he lost 6-3, 6-2. Even though he served a personal best 147 mph serve, it could not make up for his lack of movement. Schuettler, who took advantage of Roddick's bad wrist in Sydney, once again proved Roddick's master when Roddick was not quite 100 percent. After playing four matches in four days, Roddick's ankle was finally showing signs of strain.

Roddick did not use his ankle as an excuse. When asked why he was pushing off with his legs, Andy replied, "My legs were bothering me but it was no excuse because I had to deal with them all week. All credit to Schuettler." One report had Roddick using anti inflammatory on his knee and this may have been due to overcompensation because of his ankle. Andy joked to reporters that while he was injured he gained Krispy Kreme weight. Throughout the match, Andy made 28 unforced errors, twice the number as Schuettler, and had only 4 aces. Roddick's serve was not consistent and Schuettler made him pay with great passing shots.

Roddick made it to the quarter playing on one ankle with his serve dominating most of his matches. There were times when one was reminded of a young Sampras, who also played off his booming serve. Roddick was back in Florida and playing in Miami two days after Saint Patrick's Day.

Part Five: Miami Nasdaq 100

Andy Roddick's status as the King of the Serves proved to be no mirage as he prepared for the Nasdaq-100 Open in Miami. In his first 18 matches, Roddick blasted 230 aces for an average of 13 aces per match. Many of these serves speeded past the 130 mph mark. Andy took 80% of his first serves and won nearly three out of five of his second serve which allowed Andy to win 90% of his service game. Roddick was third among all male tennis players. On break points against him, Andy won 70% of those shots.

As impressive as he was in the service category, the return left a lot to be desired. The weakness Andy exhibited was in the return of service category. Andy appeared to be playing an all or nothing game. Blast and win. Andy's game seemed to rival the 2003 Boston Celtics in basketball, whose forte was the three point shot. The Celtics lived off Paul Pierce and Antoine Walker hitting three pointers. When the Celtics were hot from the outside, they won. If they were cold, they lost. When Andy's serve was on he was virtually unstoppable. When the serve was off, Andy was in trouble. So far in the season, Andy's serve was hot.

As the Ides of March passed, what became obvious was the exaggeration of the demise of American Tennis. With the just completed Indian Wells, five young Americans made it to the quarterfinals out of eight competitors. Agassi was on the sidelines with a sore shoulder and Sampras was playing Hamlet, trying to decide whether to retire or not to retire. The young lions were now ready to challenge the world.

"With Pete and Andre and [Jim] Courier all coming up together, we may never see another generation like that again," says Roddick. "But we think we have a good thing going here ourselves." Those three men and Michael Chang combined for 27 majors with Pete Sampras grabbing 14 of those. As the majors season was coming into focus, nine Americans could be seen in the top 50 and, excluding both Sampras and Agassi, the average age was 23. Roddick was the leader and already a top ten player at the age of 20. James Blake, at the age of 23, was just on the cusp of joining Andy in the top ten with Mardy Fish close to joining Blake. When you add Brian Vahaly, Taylor Dent, and Robby Ginneri—American Tennis appeared to be in good hands.

Very rarely do a Sampras and Agassi appear in the same generation. In the mid-90's, Agassi was in a prolonged slump that saw his rankings slip close to the 150 range. Most of Agassi's majors came when he was in his late 20's. To ask the present generation to match the Sampras-Agassi-Courier-Chang accomplishment was asking a lot.

Richard Pagliaro of Tennis week wrote, "The sixth-seeded Roddick looked fit when he met the media in the interview room at the Nasdaq-100 Open today. Roddick, who has come under criticism by some for being an injury-prone player, said the sheer physicality of professional tennis makes recovering from a grueling match difficult under the best of circumstances." Roddick who already suffered from a sprained ankle and wrist told reporters, "I don't know how many other sports where you're out there running side to side every point for two and a half hours with no teammates to pass the ball off to or a coach to sub someone in for you," Roddick continued that in most sports you can give all you have for two minutes and "you can call it a day."

Roddick in the early matches showed a player who was evolving from a power game to a more nuance game with different options and weapons. Roddick was no longer a player who just won on his serve. Roddick developed an aggressive baseline game, which allowed him to attack. His first opponent was qualifier Cyril Saulnier who upset Ivan Ljubicic, Roddick's conqueror in the 2002 Australian Open when Roddick had to drop out with a sprained ankle. The big serving Croatian would have been a bigger challenge than Saulnier. This looked like an easy opening match for Roddick.

Tennis matches are not played on paper and Saulnier did not roll over. Roddick prevailed though over his own sloppy shot making to defeat Saulnier in a tight three set match. He lost the first set 6-7 as Saulnier easily won the first tiebreaker 7-1. Roddick came back to win the second set through a second tiebreaker, 7-2. The third set was 2-2 when Andy finally broke through Saulnier's service game. He prevailed 6-4 in the third set and prepared himself for the veteran Todd Martin.

Todd Martin was kind of the little brother that no one paid attention to. He belonged to the same generation as Sampras and Agassi but did not share in the same Grand Slam glory as his contemporaries. The closest he ever came to winning a major was in the 1999 US Open, when he had Andre Agassi on the ropes but fell in the end. Martin demonstrated that he still had something left as he held his service in the first set. With numerous chances to break Martin's serve,

Andy could not push through and was forced into a tiebreaker. Martin won the tiebreaker 7-3.

Martin beat back the power serve of Roddick. With the score 3-3, Martin broke Roddick's serve and that was the match. He won his next serve to take a 5-3 lead. Roddick came back in the 10th game and was still within one game of tying the match. He needed to break Martin's serve, which he had yet to do. Martin took the final game and the match. Roddick's run at Miami was over in quick order.

Todd Martin looks more like a college professor out to play a friendly game than a well-trained top-notch tennis player. His graying hair hid the skills that 32-year-old still had—much to Roddick's chagrin. After the match, Martin quipped, "It (the victory) doesn't make me feel young. It just makes me feel like I can still compete and I still have a place out here."

Richard Pagliaro of Tennis Week observed, "The match up featured the old school style of Martin against one of the new ball stars in Roddick. Stylistically, it was like watching your middle-aged high school math teacher shooting set shots to beat Lebron James in a game of one-on-one." Martin could not match the firepower of Roddick but in this match—it was experience that prevailed.

Martin unexpectatedly produced more aces than Roddick, the master of the serve. When Martin had a break point, he scored. As Roddick commented, "Todd just played better on the big points."

For Roddick, this was a disappointing tournament. This was an opportunity to move up in world ranking and with Hewitt out early—a chance to even win. On this night, Todd Martin challenged Roddick and father time won.

As for Roddick, he had a rough opening match and his overall game did not match his past efforts. This was a tournament that he could easily forget.

As Andy Roddick traveled to Monte Carlo, he was still ranked number 6 in the world. Todd Martin exposed a few flaws in Roddick's game, especially the backhand groundstroke, which was still vulnerable to the better players. Originally, Monte Carlo was not on Roddick's schedule, but with injuries hampering the early part of the Tennis season, Roddick decided to use Monte Carlo as an opportunity to prepare for the French Open. Monte Carlo, like both Houston and French Open, was a clay surface.

On the other hand, Andy's strengths out numbered his weaknesses. His service appeared stronger than in previous years, and his second serve still had that extra jolt that surpassed many tennis players initial serve. And his forehand sent tennis balls streaking back in a blur.

What was becoming obvious was his ability to gut out victories even when he did not have his best game. When he overcame Cyril Saulnier in his second round win in the recent Nasdaq, it showed a maturity that was becoming obvious. Roddick's ability to overcome obstacles on the court showed that Roddick competitive nature. Great stars overcome and win, even when the best stuff is not there. This was a sign that Roddick was starting to become more complete in his game though he was not quite there.

Todd Martin said, "I think he is one of the best 10 players out here. It's just a matter of continuing to compete at the level that he's been competing at while being able to construct other areas of his game and develop into a more complete player."

If Roddick has one quality it is that he appears to have fun. On the court, his enthusiasm could be contagious as fans respond to his hand pumping and child-like appreciation of the game. For Roddick, Tennis is more sport than business, and he is having the time of his life. A reporter once wrote, "Put Roddick on a tennis court and he transforms himself from easygoing Andy into hyper competitive A-Rod who plays every point as if it's Armageddon." His Davis Cup Coach Patrick McEnroe says. "You think of Connors and the way he competed every single point. Andy's like that. He enjoys the moment, being in a big fight. 'Let's get it on.'"

There are times when on a close call, Roddick lets his opinion be known, but minus the various four letter words that occasionally left Connor's or John McEnroe's mouths. Roddick hates to lose and as McEnroe said, "You say 'Let's play a baseline game to seven and we'll work on backhands down the line,' and he'd get down and say 'Screw working on this, I want to win." It is this competitive nature that allows him to persevere.

What Roddick does have is charisma. Pete Sampras was the premier American player for the past fifteen years but was not a darling of Madison Avenue. Roddick was similar to Aggasi in that he appeared comfortable in the limelight and pressure of being America's next Tennis Superstar. At a time when Men's Tennis was disappearing from the Sports radar, Roddick was leading a new generation of Tennis stars. Roddick was made for the spotlight. Linda McIngvale, a family friend, mentioned, "Andy is a real likable kid, once you get to know him." Andy may be living in Florida but his Midwest roots shaped him and there is a "kid next door" appeal.

2

The Clay Season

Part One: Going to Monte Carlo

If Miami was a disappointment, Monte Carlo was pure disaster. One round and it was over. Roddick questioned several line calls, looked uncomfortable on the clay surface and appeared bothered by the wind. If Roddick was searching for his game, Albert Portas brought his A game to Monte Carlo. An experienced clay player, Portas used his famous drop shot (so known for his drop shot, the other players nicknamed him the drop shot dragon) and had a finer touch that kept the younger Roddick off guard.

The first set was close and decided by a tiebreaker. Portas was ranked 96th, and in a previous year was just 6-14 on clay. So how does a player like Portas come through and beat a superior Tennis player? The answer is patience. Portas allowed the game to come to him and was razor-sharp from the onset of the match. Portas's baseline volleys lured Roddick to the net, and then he popped the ball right past the rushing Roddick.

In the tiebreaker, Roddick missed a few forehands and unforced errors cost him the opening set as he was only able to gather 3 of the 10 points in the Tennis version of overtime.

Roddick appeared to be in a slump, and the next match was the Houston clay championship in which he was the favorite. If nothing else, Roddick went home with his worldwide ranking of 6 still in place. But in this match, Roddick's backhand failed him and his return of the serve was inconsistent. Roddick's ankle was still bothering him, and he did not have the explosive movement needed to return Portas's famous drop shot.

Before this match, Roddick had a chance to catch Roger Federer in the ranking wars. Federer was ahead of Andy, and this match did not help Andy to gain any ground. Plus now Roddick had to worry about Albert Costa catching him, especially if Costa won the tournament. Roddick hit a lucky break, when 16 year old Spanish player Rafeal Nadal took out Costa in the third round, securing Roddick's ranking for another week.

Roddick went back to Houston, and with his ankle less than 100 percent and his game ailing, needed to find that magic that was present in Australia.

Part Two: Houston Clay Court

Monte Carlo was one and out. Houston, however, was home to Roddick, who won the two previous Clay Court Championships. Roddick and his family lived in Austin, Texas until he was 10. Houston felt like home to Roddick. His first opponent was Jeff Morrison, the roommate of Mardy Fish. During his practice session the previous day, Morrison worked with Fish on how best to play Roddick. Unfortunately for Morrison, even with Mardy's help he was no match for Andy. Opening with a 138 mph serve, Roddick swept through the first three games before Morrison got on the board. Morrison attempted to make a game of it by splitting the next six games but Roddick prevailed in the first set, 6-3. Roddick's serve was crackling as he ended the third game with a 135 mph serve, and ended the fifth game with a 137 mph killer.

Morrison took the first game of the second set and, for one brief moment, there appeared to be a chance that a close match would happen. Roddick took his game to the next level as he swept the next six games. He broke Morrison's serve and took the fourth game with two booming serves. Roddick broke Morrison for a second time during the fifth game. He ended the sixth game with a 136 mph boomer and then broke Morrison a third time to end the match. This was a case of Roddick being at his best with the service game humming and his forehand dominating. There were occasions when the soft touch proved the right counter to the many hard balls streaming Morrison's way.

"It was nice to get your groove on American soil," Roddick told reporters after the match. He mentioned that his ankle was okay and "I make adjustments on clay vs. grass. You stand 10 feet back on grass." Roddick mentioned that he had been working more on his backhand off shot that he used in the tournament. He joked that, "I will do better in the French this year, I couldn't do worse." "Morrison would make four serves in a row and then he would miss the next few," Roddick said," I felt that I was in control in the match instead of the other way around. (referring to his previous match in Monte Carlo.)

Roddick's dominance in this game was shown in the statistics. While he had only six aces, half his average—he won over 90% of his first serves. Throughout the game, he won over 78% of his service points and even won 52% of his return services. Jeff Morrison could only manage to win 48% of his service game; demonstrating an important facet in men's tennis—lose your service game and you will lose the match.

Andy's second match was against qualifier Paul Goldstein, who previously upset Swedish player Thomas Enqvist. The wind was howling and the afternoon session was overcast. Roddick did not play his best Tennis. While he won in straight sets, he barely owned both sets 7-5 and 6-4. Goldstein, recovering from a groin injury, and ranked just a shade under 200, provided some tense moments for the Houston defending champion. Roddick, who lost to a qualifier in the first round at Monte Carlo, played tight in the opening moments of the match.

After losing the first set, Goldstein came out and rushed to a 4-2 lead in the second set. Roddick broke Goldstein in both the seventh and ninth games to grab a 5-4 lead. He closed out the set on his service game to clinch the victory. In the final game, Roddick jumped to a 40-love lead but missed the first two match points. Goldstein missed his chance to extend the match when Roddick sent a ball sailing high in the air and Goldstein whiffed on an easy overhead to end the match. Goldstein said after the match, "I have been able to stick my nose out and not been able to close the door this year." Goldstein had his chance to beat Roddick but could not take advantage of his opportunities.

"I had to fight the wind as much as Goldstein," Roddick said, "I rely a lot on my serve and the wind was blowing the toss around a little bit." Roddick added, "I take pretty big cuts at the ball and that doesn't help either, but luckily I was able to bear down when I needed to and win the big points." Fiona Simon, internet tennis reporter, commented that Goldstein reminded her of Michael Chang. Running down every ball and fighting to the end.

Roddick's service game was not sharp as he was broken in the fourth game of the first set, but he broke Goldstein in the seventh and eleventh games of the first set, and that proved to be the difference. Roddick lost 23 points on his service game but Goldstein lost 34. In his match with Morrison, Roddick rarely lost a service game winning 90% of his service points.

Roddick's next match was with the Brazilian Fernando Meligeni, whom he had previously split with in their last two matches. Roddick took the first set 6-3 and was up by a break in the second set when Meligeni broke Roddick twice and took the second set 6-4. With the match even, Roddick appeared down and Meligeni had the momentum for a big upset.

Going into the final set, Roddick needed to break Meligeni while holding his own. This he did as he overtook the stubborn Brazilian.

In the semis, Roddick squared off against French tennis player, Olivier Mutis. The set was nip and tuck as Roddick looked uncomfortable with Mutis matching Roddick serve for serve. In the ninth game, Mutis broke through and broke Roddick to take a 5-4 lead in the first set. Mutis then proceeded to serve out the game. Roddick's frustration was demonstrated when he threw his racket at his seat after the set.

The second set began with a few big serves as Roddick opened up a 1-0 lead. He finally broke the Frenchman in the second game and now found himself up 2-0. He took his next service game and Mutis would only take the fourth game as Roddick recovered his rhythm. In the final set Roddick broke Mutis to take a 2-1 lead. In the fifth game and down double break point, Mutis held on to his serve and trailed 3 games to 2. Andy, in the seventh game, broke Mutis a second time in the set taking a 5-2 lead with his service game to wrap up. Roddick zipped out to a 30-0 lead and then closed out the show with his fastest serve, 140 mph. Andy was now in the finals for the third time in a row.

Roddick told reporters, "I was thinking if I could get off to a quick start, it's going to work on his mental thinking about three sets, thinking about the heat more, his legs more." Roddick was going to turn this match into an alley fight.

After the match, Mutis said, "He has a terrific first serve, but what surprised me was his second serve. It was more difficult to return than his first serve. His second serve has an unbelievable kick."

The finals featured Andy Roddick against Andre Agassi. Agassi, at the age of 33, was playing the best Tennis of his life and with his semifinal win at Houston would take over the number one ranking. For Roddick, this was his first big test against one of the elites of Tennis.

Roddick came out fast and Agassi seemed lethargic. Andy broke Agassi's service game in the eighth game, as Andre made too many unforced errors. Roddick won the first set 6-3. This was the first time Roddick had ever won a set off Agassi in an ATP event. The two have played twice in charity exhibitions; both times Roddick winning in straight sets. The last time they played in actual competition, Agassi completely humiliated Roddick with a 6-3, 6-1 win in San Jose in 2002. The second set started like the first. Roddick immediately broke Agassi to take the lead and gave himself the opportunity for another break in the third game. Roddick was up triple break point when Agassi rallied, and the momentum changed as Agassi took over. Agassi woke up and started to work the lines, pounding away at Roddick. In the eighth game, Agassi broke Roddick's serve for the first time in the match zipping back four returns and shutting Roddick out on Andy's serve. Agassi finished by breaking Roddick in the ninth game winning the second set 6-3.

Roddick began the third game serving with the goal of trying to regain the momentum that he had in the first game. In the fifth game, Andy nailed a 131 mph serve, but it was Andre who delivered on two-drop shots and one deep return to break serve. Andre began to play the angles, dropping shots and taking the best that Andy had to offer. Andre was being Andre, and Roddick's game was good enough to beat most anybody but Andre, who was like a surgeon on a roll. Agassi took the sixth game and moved out to a 4-2 lead. Roddick defended his serve in the seventh and ninth games. Agassi now needed to serve to end this struggle. Four straight points including an ace ended it. Agassi won the Houston clay court championship by taking the final set, 6-4, and Roddick lost his bid at a third straight Houston Clay championship. Agassi proved to be the master still, not quite ready to surrender his number one ranking. Roddick showed that he was getting close to the elites of the game but was not quite there. He is on the way though, and the old masters will someday be gone with Andy taking his place at the top.

After the match, Roddick said, "Andre is the greatest player, I had to take chances with him." Agassi said, "Andy kept me from getting comfortable, and I had a bit of luck." Agassi stated that he was ready for the French Open. Roddick felt that he was also ready for Roland Garros.

Part Three: Touring New York

The life of a superstar goes beyond what goes on in the court. Your time is not always your own. In the 24 hours after Houston, Andy flew to New York to appear on the popular Regis and Kelly show. Regis Philben and Kelly Ripa dominated the 9 pm slot with a combination of Regis's humor, Kelly's narratives of her family life (though not to the extent of Kelly's predecessor, Kathy Lee Gifford), and guests often selling their books or movies. On some occasions the guest will be asked to do some entertaining chore. Andy appeared as the last guest, after actor Matt Dillon was shown selling his latest movie.

Regis introduced Andy, "Here is one of Tennis's sexiest stars, and I am not talking the Williams sisters and the Russian girl, I'm talking Andy Roddick." Andy entered the room and sat on a breakfast chair.

Regis began with a whopper of a mistake as he asked what it was like to play "Alex" when he meant Andre Agassi. He quickly recovers and says, "Andre." Kelly began the questioning by asking, "What is like to play a legend like Andre?"

Andy replied, "I have been on the tour for three years and the awe is fading." Andy added, "I was just five years old when Andre won this tournament for the first time." Kelly, moving quickly, asked, "Did you mention this to him?" Andy grinned, "No, but some one at the press conference did."

Andy then introduced actress-singer Mandy Moore, his girlfriend, and sheepishly says, "This is more serious than in the past," when asked by Regis how serious their relationship was. (Andy did not look all that comfortable talking about their relationship.) Mandy and Andy have been seeing each other for nine months and while both lead public lives, they prefer quiet evenings watching movies at home. That is, when they can be together, since Tennis and Hollywood have both on the road much of the time.

Regis asked Andy, "Can you play ping pong?" Andy, smiling slowly, replied, "I will try." Regis laughs and tells the audience that Andy's answer means Regis is about to be taken.

They went on to play table tennis joking and laughing as Andy "beats" Regis 5-4. After the show, it was off to Rock n' Rally, which was the USTA tennis event to promote Tennis on a grass roots level and to sell US Open tickets. He left with Mandy, and his sister-in-law and publicist, Ginger, for the Rockefeller Center and the Rock'n'Rally event. The ice-skating rink was transformed into a tennis court. Andy was at the event along with James Blake, female tennis player Alexandra Stevenson, Jim Courier, Pat McEnroe and Zina Garrison.

Before the event, the press interviewed each player. Rock and roll played in the background as the event unfolded. Andy teamed with Alexandra Stevenson vs. Jim Courier and Zina Garrison. Andy and Alexandra won the game, but during the game there was a little brinkmanship, as McEnroe yelled at Roddick, "Come on Andy, show them your real serve!" Andy looked at Jim and served him the Andy special. Courier missed as the serve hit his frame and the ball flew out of the rink. After this match James Blake and Andy Roddick hit at each other but mostly they were just playing for fun. James hit one shot between the leg and another behind the back overhead return.

Part Four: Rome

Andy Roddick began his warm-up for the French Open by playing in the Rome clay tournament championship. After his second place finish in Houston, Roddick began the European clay season with confidence. His opening match in Rome was against Italy's Andrea Gaudenzi. For Roddick who had never won a tournament outside the United States, this could prove to be the right opportunity. He began with a smooth performance, winning 6-2, 6-3. In the first set, Roddick broke Gaudenzi's serve to take a 4-2 lead and then broke Gaudenzi a second time to win the first set. As easy as this set appeared to be, Andy couldn't afford to be sanguine. The number one seed and defending champion, Andre Agassi easily won his first set against David Ferrer 6-0, but Ferrer came back to win a tie breaker to tie the match, and then won the third set 6-4 for the big upset.

Roddick began the second set as he did the first, staying on serve. Roddick's service game was good, but in the second set Gaudenzi was having better luck in picking up the serve. Until the eighth game, both players held serve. Roddick slipped past Gaudenzi on Gaudenzi's service game to take a 5-3 lead and then Roddick served out the victory.

This game was vintage Roddick, holding the serve and using powerful forehand serve returns to break service. Roddick's next opponent was the 6'6" Dutch giant Martin Verkerk. These two men scored 557 aces over the year. Aces settled this particular match, with Verkerk scoring 22. Verkerk also consistently returned Roddick's serves and rallied with his groundstrokes.

The last time these two men played each other was the first round of the US Open, Andy winning in straight sets. On clay, it was the Dutch who returned the favor by winning the final two sets 6-3 and 6-4 after losing the first in a tiebreaker. Roddick showed his frustration hitting a ball into the stands, for which he was warned.

Neither man could break the other's service game in the first set, though Roddick prevailed in an 8-6 tiebreaker. Roddick opened the second set breaking Verkerk's serve, but Verkerk took Roddick's advantage back in the next game and broke Roddick a second time in the sixth game taking a 4-2 lead.

Verkerk broke Roddick's serve in the fifth game in the third set and went on to win the match. Verkerk's game was built for Wimbledon with a big serve that was perfect for grass, and while others prepared for the French open, Verkerk was looking toward Wimbledon. Having never played on grass, Verkerk felt that he had the game for Wimbledon, and beating Roddick demonstrated that he could be competitive at Wimbledon, his 68th world ranking not withstanding. And Verkerk beat Roddick on his strength. So how does the 68th ranked player upset the world's 6th best? It is the depth of men's tennis.

After the match, Verkerk said, "the way he (Roddick) plays with the crowd and tries to impress upon people that he is Andy Roddick who has big game." Verkerk enjoyed the emotion that Roddick puts in his game but he added, "We were fighting, man-to-man, and I won."

After the match, Roddick said, "I played a sloppy service game early in the second set. After that, he started playing really well." Roddick added, "the way he returned and was hitting winners with his ground-strokes was really impressive." When asked about grass and Wimbledon, Verkerk said, "I've never played on grass before in my life. I'm playing Rosmalen and Wimbledon for the first time." Verkerk added, "I'm looking forward to it, but I always thought it would be tough for me to play on grass because I'm pretty big to get to low shots, and my knees were not always as strong as they are now."

Roddick, showing his eye for stats, told reporters that Verkerk "had a plus 22 winner to error ratio, so that's not so bad." When asked if the clay in Rome was different than in Houston, Roddick responded, "Little bit, not too much. Nothing that will affect my preparation." Roddick admitted that Verkerk was a better player than when they met at the US Open. Rome was filled with upsets starting with Agassi, and as Roddick commented, "We play 40-something weeks a year, it's bound to happen at a tournament that all the top players go out some time." As shocking as the result was, Verkerk's run in Rome was a precursor to his success at Roland Garros. He would make it to the finals with wins over former French Open champ, Carlos Moya and Guillermo Coria before losing to Spain's Juan Carlos Ferrero. The Dutch man would have a game for Wimbledon but he showed the skill to play on clay.

Roddick concluded that Verkerk's ability to hit to his return and groundstrokes were the deciding factor in the game. This match affected Roddick's world 6th place ranking and now Roddick was facing an uphill battle to maintain his place in the world's top 8.

Part Five: Roddick at Hamburg

Andy Roddick opened up the Hamburg Open by defeating Ivan Ljubicic 6-4, 6-4 as the Clay season continued. In the first set, Roddick and Ljubicic were even at 3-3. Ljubicic defended his serve in the seventh game and Roddick defended his in the eighth, and it was looking like a tiebreaker. Finally, in the ninth game, Roddick broke serve and in the tenth game, Roddick nailed his serve and the set was over.

The second set began just like the first with each player holding serve. Ljubicic smacked a big serve to go up 3-2 and Roddick matched Ivan's big service in the sixth game. Finally in the seventh game, Roddick broke Ljubicic's game and served out the eighth game to take a 5-3 game. Roddick's service game was on target, and during the 10th game Roddick held serve and moved on to the second round.

Roddick now went on to play Argentinean Agustin Calleri taking deep breaths as he adjusted his hat before serving the opening volley. Roddick served to begin the game and released his usual collection of accurate booming serves. Calleri couldn't return and Roddick opened up with a 1-0 lead.

Roddick took the second game as he broke Calleri's serve early in the match. Roddick's service game was in fine form as he raced to a 3-0 lead. After the fifth game, Calleri was down 4-1 with Roddick looking for the kill. Calleri kept hitting to Roddick's forehand and receiving missiles back. He was playing Roddick's game.

While Calleri won the sixth game, Roddick served out the seventh game smashing a service that went 205 km/h. Calleri could barely get his racket on the ball, and Roddick was in control. While Calleri took the eighth game to stay competitive, Roddick hit 40-0 before Calleri could even touch the ball, and Roddick won the first set 6-3.

Calleri took the first game of the second set and Roddick the second. The Argentinean at this point had twice as many unforced errors and the pressure was building. Calleri needed one break or this was going to be a short night. In the third game, Calleri started to move Roddick side to side, and Roddick hit the net on his forehand as Calleri took the third game.

During the fourth game, Calleri started to hit Roddick's serve back, and Roddick started to miss on his first serve. One last force error allowed Calleri to break serve and from this point on the Argentinean had the momentum. Calleri, using brawn, started serving to Roddick's backhand and won the fifth game, though Roddick held serve to keep the set competitive. During the seventh game, Calleri took his time and took an easy 40-15 lead, as he was out volleying the young American. He served out the game and now was one game from winning the set.

Roddick had to hold serve to stay in the game but his serve was betraying him. Calleri, counterpunching to Roddick's backhand, nailed a perfect shot down the line and suddenly was one point away from emerging victorious. Finally, one last Roddick unforced error ended the set. Throughout the second set, Roddick missed on two-thirds of his first serve and Calleri started to smack Roddick's forehand, while Roddick's groundstrokes were flying out of the court. Roddick's game started to become wild.

Calleri began the third set with confidence, and was now rivaling the pace of Roddick's service game. Calleri was getting his serve in and ended the first game with an ace. Roddick held serve and it was now tied.

Calleri smacked a backhand down the line to end the third game and pumped his fist in the direction of his coach. Roddick was reeling though the match was still up for grabs. Roddick began the fourth game by getting his first serve in and aiming for the wide corner of the court. He won the fourth game and once again Calleri held on to his service game in the fifth.

In the sixth game, Roddick nailed the first point as Calleri's shot hit the net. But Calleri returned Roddick's next serve with a drop shot, and suddenly Roddick found himself dropping the next three points, and lost his service game. Roddick kicked up the clay, as he looked frustrated.

Calleri easily took the seventh game and Roddick looked shell-shocked. While Roddick defended his service game in the eighth game, Calleri was now serving for the match. It did not look good for the fourth seeded player. Even in his victorious service game, he double faulted three times but managed to pull it out.

Calleri opened up the ninth game and his first serve came back quickly as he lost the first point. He then smashed two serves and took a 30-15. Calleri was two match points from victory. Next serve produced another Calleri point. Calleri finished this match with an ace.

Roddick lost his composure in the second and third sets and Calleri took advantage of every Roddick unforced error. Out in the second set, Roddick had one more tune up in Austria before the French Open coming up in two weeks. Roddick dropped 12 out of the 17 final games played in the final two sets after winning the first set 6-3. The final score card read 6-3, 2-6, 3-6.

Part Six: Roddick in Austria

After slumping on European clay, Roddick was hoping to use Saint Pölten to recapture the momentum he received after finishing second to Agassi in Houston. Since leaving Houston, Roddick was 2-3 in Monte Carlo, Rome and Hamburg and had yet to make it beyond the second round. Memories of last year's French Open in which Roddick was eliminated in the first round were still raw.

Roddick started the Saint Pölten tournament with a 6-1, 7-6 victory over Spain's Alberto Martin. After the match, Roddick said, "I am already playing good tennis. Now I have to cross the line and start winning, too. If I can win here it will give me a huge boost in self-confidence for Paris."

Philipp Kohlschreiber was Andy's next opponent. Kohlschreiber had to qualify to get to the first round and now was facing the number 4 seed. Through the fifth game, both men were on the serve before Roddick broke through. With the score 4-2, Roddick served out the seventh game to take a 5-2 lead. While Kohlschreiber held serve in the eighth game, Roddick finished out the ninth game and won 6-3.

Roddick opened up the second set as he did the first, winning the opening game on serve. During the second game, Andy broke Kohlschreiber's serve and, from this point on, Roddick held all of his service game and won the second set 6-4, and the match. Roddick's serve and forehand worked in synergistic fashion as he looked impressive marching into the quarterfinals against the hard-hitting Richard Krajicek.

Krajicek beat American Brian Vahaly, 6-2, 2-6, 6-3 and this promised to be a battle of Tennis's two bigger bangers. Krajicek was one of the game's most potent servers, so Roddick was prepared for a battle of serves.

Krajicek's career highlight was the 1996 Wimbledon when he downed Malivai Washington in straight sets to win the championship. Krajicek, was a hard server, and had been a top ten player for the past several years.

Roddick dominated the match as his sizzling forehand complimented his powerful serve. In just over one hour, Roddick moved one step closer to his first tournament win outside the United States. 10 years younger than Krajicek, Roddick was never in any danger of losing. "He was a top ten player for years so I knew I had to play well to beat him," Roddick said after the match, "My forehand was good today—I could control the points from the baseline and I returned well, so I think that was the key."

While Roddick was wrapping up his game 7-5, 6-1 in surprisingly easy fashion, Spanish David Sanchez was defeating the Croatian youngster Mario Ancic. The semifinals were now set and Roddick was two matches away from nabbing the tournament. Loving Austria on his first trip, Roddick said, "I've never been here to Austria before, but it's a really nice center court and they have great Wiener Schnitzel here." Roddick was feeling comfortable at Saint Pölten, and now was ever closer to his first international victory.

Between the blisters on his feet and the sweltering serve of Roddick, Sanchez was doomed. Roddick rolled through the first set easily winning 6-2. The eighth seed Sanchez retired from the match as the blisters prevented him from playing effectively. Now Roddick was one match away from his first victory outside the States.

To win this title, he must first beat Nikolay Davydenko. The sixth seeded Russian eliminated Martin Verkerk, Roddick's conqueror in Rome, in two sets 7-5, 6-1. Verkerk, like Roddick, possessed a powerful serve and Davydenko was able to beat him easily. Roddick's serve was crackling and his forehand dominant. He took three out of the first four games and now was on his way to winning the first set.

Davydenko won the sixth game as he defended serve and Roddick took the seventh game. Down 5-2, Davydenko once again prevailed in his service game, though Roddick ended the first set with four sizzling serves. First set 6-3.

Andy won the first game of the second set just as he had the first set, 1-0. Roddick breezed through the first three games before Davydenko won a game in the set. Roddick had momentum and now smelled his first international victory. Davydenko was helpless against the onslaught. Roddick was on a roll and Davydenko could not prevail. The second set ended 6-2 and Roddick was hoisting the winner's trophy.

After the match, Roddick told reporters, "I felt good out there and it's great to be in the final here before Paris." Roddick added, "It's a little bit of a monkey off my back. I've never played as well in Europe as I have in the States, so it's definitely nice to get my first win here" Davydenko was having his best year, and yet, Roddick found a way to win. This was not an easy match or easy tournament. For the past several weeks Roddick had been slumping, losing more than he was winning on his European circuit. Now, he was ready for Paris. The French Open was just two days away and Roddick was ready for the next major.

Part Seven: Final Drama on Clay—Roddick in Paris

Roland Garros. The Red Clay of Roland Garros stands alone in the majors. The hard courts are routine in the United States and every tennis buff plays their weekend tennis on hard court. Clay represented a European touch and the surface's distinctive color reminds one of the red planet Mars. Clay—the red surface of Mars transported through space onto Roland Garros. For many Americans, Roland Garros seemed alien. Roddick did not even make it out of the first round last year and Sampras never could conquer the Red Clay of Roland Garros. It was the one surface that bedeviled the greatest tennis player in the opens era.

Roland Garros was where dreams are made and broken. There were no favorites, only survivors, as this tricky surface required sliding skills as much as it did a good forehand or backhand. Of all of the surfaces, Roland Garros evened up the field and those who would normally be favored at Wimbledon or the US Open may find themselves sightseeing in Paris early.

Lleyton Hewitt had the tenacity, and physical stamina to play clay but this was one tournament that he never did well in. And yet, there were changes happening on the clay surface. In the early 90's, Roland Garros was home to defensive specialists, who could take advantage of the slow surface to bewilder the stars. Now the clay specialist was slowing fading away. With new technology and training techniques, the stars slowly started taking command of the surface.

In the year 2003, Clay surface has lost its mystique, and Roland Garros was ready to be taken on by the right American. Andre Agassi had won at Roland Garros in 1999 and, at the age of 33, he was as fit and strong as he had ever been in his career. Last year, he lost in the Quarterfinals to Ferrero, who used his youth and speed as an advantage. Agassi was as smart a player as any in the game today, and savvy was his chief weapon. The youthful James Blake had the forehand and defense to win on clay though some questioned his service game. The leading challenger included defending champion Albert Costa, Roger Federer, and Juan Carlos Ferrero, the loser to Costa in 2002 French Open, and Ferrero was considered one of the world's best players on clay. Lleyton Hewitt had the wheels and tenacity, but some questioned his power even though he was the world's best player. And of course, Brazilian Kuerten's reputation began in Roland Garros.

Roddick has played well on clay in spurts with two straight Houston victories, and the previous week won on the clay of Saint Pölten. Roddick was ready to reverse last year's first round loss. Roddick had received a pretty decent draw, if he could take advantage of it. He wouldn't run into a true "dirtballer" until the round of 16, where Fernando Gonzalez awaited him.

Roddick opened up his Paris campaign against Sargis Sargsian. Sargsian had lots of experience but was not known for his clay court play. Sargsian began the game countering Roddick's game with a smooth groundstroke. Roddick took the first set with a 7-3 victory in the tiebreaker. The first set was too close and now Sargis Sargsian had confidence that he could play with the young Americans.

Sargsian was a regular practice partner of Andre Agassi and had more Grand Slam experience than his younger American opponent. Even though he only reached the 4th round once in 25 Grand Slams, Sargsian was a quality competitor who could play spirited Tennis.

In the second set, he broke Roddick in the second game and consolidated his lead in the third game. The third game ended with a weak Roddick return into the net and Roddick's racket hit the ground with extreme force as the frustrated Roddick looked bewildered. Sargsian, noticing the frustration on Roddick's face, worked the angles and, like a prizefighter, used these angles to force Roddick into awkward spots on the court. Sargsian had shown a capacity to beat the power hitters in the past and, his ability to take the charge of Roddick's serve earlier gave him all the advantage of the baseline exchanges. Roddick chose to return from far behind the baseline, giving up most of the court to Sargsian, allowing him to find the angles and control the points.

Over the next three sets, Sargsian managed to break Roddick six times. Roddick only took three out of the next fifteen games in set two and three as Sargsian dominated. In the fourth set, Roddick began to dig in as he started to match Sargsian's baseline. The game appeared within reach as Roddick managed to break Sargsian's serve once, but this was a mere illusion as Sargsian gathered his break back and finished out the young American in the fourth set, 6-4. For the second year in a row, Roddick left Paris early, joined by most of his male American teammates, as only Agassi managed to survive the first week. The clay court of Roland Garros sent the Americans reeling, and if not for Agassi, no American would have made the quarters. Agassi in his second match was down 2 sets to Love to Mario Ancic but, unlike Roddick, he kept his cool and pulled that game out. Agassi, the old lion of American Tennis, still had the skills and experience to play with the best. The divide that separated Agassi from his younger American teammates still proved wide.

Many of Andy's fans show their appreciation during one of his practices in Cincinnati.

Andy Roddick practicing that fearsome forehand.

Roddick getting ready to return.

Andy's fans watching a practice session.

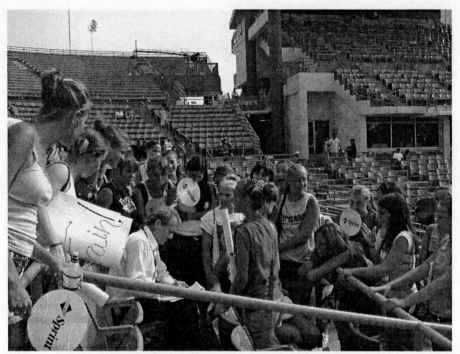

Author Tom Donelson chatting with Andy's fans.

Author Beth Donelson queuing with Roddick's fans in Wimbledon.

The authors with Andy Roddick's parents, Blanche and Jerry.

Andy Roddick and Mardy Fish strategizing between sets at a doubles match during the Houston Clay Courts Championship.

Author Beth Donelson and Andy Roddick after the 2002 Davis Cup competition in Paris.

3

The Grass Season

Part One: Switching Coaches

Even though he told reporters in his post match interview, "my coach didn't lose the match. You know, he's smart. I'm the one losing the matches. He's not losing them. You know, when we're doing well, we're the perfect fit and we've been together for four years," Roddick decided to make a change. His first round loss at the French Open indicated stagnation. A week later Tarik Benhabiles was out and Brad Gilbert was in. Tarik and Andy had been together for four years. They first met on one rainy day in Kalamazoo, Michigan, during a rain delay at the Junior Championships. Tarik was taking shelter under the same canopy as Blanche Roddick and, after a few pleasantries and a conversation, they found out that not only do they both live in Boca Raton, Florida, but were neighbors as well. The meeting may have happened by chance but it was clear that it was meant to be. Benhabiles, who had previously worked with other pros Nicolas Escude and Cedric Pioline, had been looking for the right young player to take on as his new charge. Andy and Tarik were the perfect match for each other.

Unlike Andy, Tarik was not a power player in his day. A perennial top 30 player, reaching as high as 22 in the world, Tarik had to use everything in his 5'9" frame. Andy once remarked that he thought Tarik always had fun teaching what he never had. Born in Algiers, Algeria, Tarik played under the French flag and was more a clay court player than a hard court player like Andy. His best showing in a grand slam was his round 16 loss to Mats Wilander. Tarik was not a player who could out power anyone on a serve but was pesky nonetheless. Tarik brought more to Andy's game than just coaching and contrasts. He also brought a real friendship. Andy told French Tennis Magazine in 2002, "He's my best friend; he's part of my family now."

Within a few months of working with each other Andy went from being just another player in the juniors to the top. In December of 1999, Andy won the prestigious Orange Bowl, which gave him an automatic wildcard into the Ericsson Open, now the Nasdaq-100 in Miami. He then followed this victory up by winning the Australian Open Juniors Championships and the US Open Juniors Championships in September of 2000. Under Tarik's tutelage Andy began to see his own talent and decided to bypass college and try his hand as a pro. It became clear that it was a wise decision. Andy started the 2001-year with a win as a challenger in Hawaii, but it was his win over Pete Sampras at the 2001 Ericsson Open that announced to the world that he could be the next great American Champion.

It wasn't just the results that brought the two together, but their relationship off the court as well. Some players' relationships with their coaches are only business. They meet at practice and at tournaments and that's it. Andy and Tarik were family. They would have breakfast together and spend holidays together. Tarik was more then just a coach, he was a best friend and a second father. Despite their different personalities, they made it work. Andy's more outgoing and Tarik's more reserved. At times Tarik was the calming influence on Andy.

Andy and Tarik had a successful first full year on the ATP tour in 2001. At this point, everything Andy did, was eaten up by the media. He couldn't do anything wrong. At the 2001 US Open Andy made it to the quarterfinals and had a classic match with the eventual US Open champion, Lleyton Hewitt. Andy matched Hewitt shot for shot. At 4-5 down, Andy exploded when the umpire, Jorge Diaz, overruled a line call that Andy felt was in. Unable to control his temper he lost his serve as well as the match. Andy would have to go home and watch Hewitt demolish Pete Sampras in the finals to win the US Open. It was a bitter pill to swallow, and the media began to question whether Andy had the mind of a champion. Despite winning two tournaments and ending the year in the top 10 for the first time, it wasn't the last of the criticism. According to the media, he failed when it came to the big stage. This criticism continued throughout the 2002 season, even though Andy finished in the top ten once again.

Calls for a new coach started, with several rumors floating around that Andy and Tarik had split, but they continued to work together. The 2003 season started off well with Andy making his first semifinals at a Grand Slam at the Australian Open, but a couple of minor injuries and some less then spectacular results in the tournaments leading up to the French Open, put Tarik back in the hot seat. The final straw came when Andy lost in the first round of the French Open for the second year in a row. He had just won a title on clay the week before in St. Poelten but just looked lost against Sargis Sargsian. The chorus for Andy to get rid of Tarik was louder than ever. Even Mary Carillo, ESPN analyst and former pro went so far as to shout out for Gilbert to give Andy a call after the loss, but Andy wouldn't hear of it or was just ready for the move. But Carillo was right, the move was near.

It must have been the longest train ride from Paris to London in Andy's life because he knew what he had to do. Andy was going to tell Tarik in person that he was going in a different direction. A week later, news broke that Andy and Tarik had split. In his official statement, Andy said, "I credit Tarik with my success. However, it has come to a time in my growth and development that I need a fresh voice." And with that, their professional relationship was over.

With Tarik now gone, Andy was in need of a new coach. While the rest of the tennis world was still watching the final week of the French Open, they were also keeping a close eye on whom Andy would pick for his new coach. It was widely rumored that Brad Gilbert would get the call though Andy had trouble getting through. His first attempt to call Gilbert ended up with being hung up on by Gilbert's youngest daughter, Zoe. Andy was on a mission though for a new coach, and being hung up on by a six year old would not deter him. Two more calls and a short conversation later, Brad was on a plane to London to work with Andy.

If you call Tarik soft spoken, it is definitely safe to say that Brad Gilbert is out spoken. Gilbert will have no problem giving you a piece of his mind. The trick with him is to get him to stop talking. The author of the highly popular book, *Winning Ugly*, probably is the best way to describe the kind of tennis he played. Like Tarik, Gilbert was not blessed with the physical talent of Andy but used what he had to win matches. In his case, he used his mind. Known to be a tactical genius, he threw in everything but the kitchen sink to reach a ranking high of number 4 in 1990. In the summer of 1989, Gilbert won over 20 matches going into the US Open, only to lose in the first round.

What Gilbert did as a player was completely overshadowed by his accomplishments as a coach. In 1994, he teamed up with Andre Agassi. With his long, blond hair and neon shorts, Agassi got a lot of attention but mostly for off court activities. He was seen as more flash than substance. He did manage to win Wimbledon before he started to work with Gilbert, but it was under his tutelage that Agassi became the Champion that he is today. He instilled a work ethic in Agassi that wasn't there before, and Agassi went on to win six more Grand Slams. They worked together for eight years, in what has got to be called the most successful player/coach relationship in the history of tennis. In less than a year, Andre went from the top 30 to number 1 in the world.

Gilbert, not one to keep his expertise from the masses, published his book *"Winning Ugly: The Mental Warfare of Tennis"* with co-author Steve Jamison. It has become one of the best selling tennis books of all times and has been published in several different countries and several languages.

After eight years, six grand slams, and an Olympic Gold Medal, Gilbert and Agassi went their separate ways in early 2002. Agassi benefited from Lleyton Hewitt's firing of Coach Darren Cahill and immediately hired him while Gilbert decided it was time for a break. He went back to Southern California to be with his family. Occasionally players would fly to work with him there. Croatian star Mario Ancic was one of the many players who worked with Gilbert. He also continued to write his guest columns for the newspaper USA Today, and made appearances on Sports Shows to keep himself busy between coaching Jobs. After such a successful partnership with Andre, not just any player would do for Gilbert. Like Gilbert told Tennis Week Magazine in June of 2003, "I was looking for the right young person with a lot of talent. Phil Jackson waited for the Lakers. He didn't come back to coach the Warriors." In late May of '03, Gilbert got his wish. He got the call from Andy and the next day was on a plane to London to meet him.

Part two: Gilbert Age begins at Queens

The grass season began with turmoil. Andy Roddick parted from his coach of three years, Tarik Benhabiles and hired Brad Gilbert. Gilbert aided Andre Agassi's rise to the top and now was hoping to impose his magic on Roddick. As a player Gilbert captured 15 single titles but no major. He was better known for being Agassi's coach and his book, "Winning Ugly," which detailed the strategic aspects of Tennis.

Roddick's first match under Gilbert was against South African Rik De Voest. As Gilbert watched his new protégé, Roddick started out strong. All match long, he was zipping some of the fastest serves ever seen on grass. Roddick was nailing serves in the mid 140s and easily prevailed over De Voest, 6-3, 6-2. Roddick took a 4-2 lead in the first set when he first broke DeVoest with a wicked crosscourt forehand passing shot that was out of De Voest's reach.

Roddick was cautious at the beginning of the match until his first break and from that point on he took command of the game. Roddick told reporters, "I didn't know much about him, but he had won four matches in a row so you have to be kind of wary of him."

When asked about his footing on grass, Andy replied, "the footing was fine, these are great grass courts, uh, I made a couple too many errors that I didn't like in the first set, a couple of balls I maybe shouldn't have missed." Roddick added that he found his groove in the second set. The first test of the Gilbert era was over and Roddick passed.

Greg Rusedski was Roddick's next opponent. This was the battle of two of the biggest boomers in Tennis. Roddick had the second fastest recorded serve, Rusedski being the man with the record. Plus Grass was Rusedski's favorite surface. As Brad Falkner of Tennis Week wrote, "Shooting out serves at such speed the balls looked like BB's, the two gunslingers split the first two sets." The crowd favored British player Rusedski, and were certainly treated to a tremendous match. With the services game blistering the court, the match was three fast-paced sets, and even in the last set, the match was in doubt.

In the first set, Rusedski and Roddick held serve until the sixth game when Roddick broke Rusedski with some baseline plays and forehand shots. Roddick was also nailing his serve in the mid 140's and Rusedski was not just in danger of losing the game, but possibly losing his record as the games hardest server. In the seventh game Roddick continued his onslaught as he closed out Rusedski and took control of the set. The first set went Roddick's way.

The second set started out in Rusedski's favor as he swept the first three games. Roddick held serve in the fourth game and with some sizzling returns, Roddick broke Rusedski to get back in the game, 2-3. Roddick's serve allowed him to win the game and tie the set. Rusedski's service game came back in the seventh game, and now it appeared that maybe, the second set was headed for a tiebreaker.

Roddick's own booming serve allowed him to tie the set and Rusedski shot his way back into the lead in the very next game. Down by one game in the set, Andy sought to tie the set up. Rusedski's returns put pressure on the young American, and he broke Roddick's serve a second time to take the set. The match was now tied one set apiece with the third deciding set still to come.

Rusedski took the first game easily as Roddick appeared to lose focus. Roddick countered in the second game with some booming serves of his own. The match was dead even.

This set became a match of big serves as Rusedski easily served out the third game but Roddick held serve to tie the set. In the fifth game, Roddick nailed a backhand to tie the game and nearly took over the match as he missed a forehand by inches off a wicked Rusedski serve. Rusedski served out the game, won, and took a 3-2 lead in the set. Roddick nailed a few forehands to tie the set. Rusedski with the game tied at 30-30 pitched a perfect serve and once again Rusedski was ahead. Once again, a tiebreaker appeared on the horizon as Roddick won the game. The ninth game began with Rusedski rushing to a 40-15 lead. Rusedski hit the next shot in the net and the game concluded with a Rusedski volley back in the net. Roddick now held a 5-4 lead in the final set and all he had to do was hold serve. And that is exactly what he did as he won the set and the match 6-4.

After the match Roddick told the media, "I thought I was hitting my returns a little better and it showed today." Against Rusedski, Roddick played a good game with the exception of the two-service game he lost in the second set. When asked the one difference what was in his victory, Roddick said, "I was making my passing shots. I was getting a high percentage of serves in." Roddick showed improvement in his backhand and this, too, was a factor in his win.

Roddick's next opponent was Taylor Dent who defeated Roddick easily in the Memphis final. Roddick said of his close friend, "Taylor is at home on the grass, it's probably his best surface…He's probably got a better game for it." This was Dent's first Queen's club quarterfinal. Brad Gilbert decided that Roddick should give up his Reebok visor, for as Roddick quipped, "He said it is not intimidating enough and I couldn't really argue with him. I couldn't really come up with a quick one liner back." Brad Gilbert wears a black hat sporting the logo of the heavy-metal group Metallica and Roddick joked, "you can't exactly say that Metallica is for wussies."

Andy Roddick faced off against Taylor Dent. Roddick was on his game in the first match, breaking Taylor Dent twice and took an easy 6-3 first set. The second set became a game of matching serves. Neither player could break the other and the game was settled in a tiebreaker. Roddick said after the match, "This is Taylor's best surface, He's almost boring to play on this stuff, with his attacking style. I knew if I wanted to win that I would have to take some chances." Roddick ran away with the tiebreaker 7-3 and now was facing Andre Agassi in the semifinals. Roddick had faced Agassi four times and came away on the short end, four times. "We played a pretty good match in Houston so coming here pretty soon after that it's exciting…The last time we played I was pretty close to winning. I had him on the ropes a little bit," Roddick said when asked his thoughts of a fifth meeting with Agassi.

At this point in the tournament, Roddick's extra practice on grass was paying off as he practiced conscientiously on grass surfaces. His goal was to erase the disappointment of losing in the first round at Paris.

Roddick then faced Andre Agassi for the second time within two months. In his first match of the 2003 season, he won the first set easily before succumbing to the more experienced Agassi. Now it was the semifinals of the Queens and only Andre Agassi stood between Roddick and the finals. Roddick won the opening set easily just as he had in Houston during the Clay finals. "I was flawless in the first set," Roddick recalled after the match. Roddick was producing sensational serves including a record tying fast serve at 149 mph and aced Agassi 27 times in the three set match. Aggasi was unfazed at the bullets coming his way as he held his serve in the second set and forced a tiebreaker. Agassi took the tiebreaker 7-5 and now it appeared that history was about to repeat itself.

Roddick was facing another defeat at the hands of his chief American nemesis and the man who was now king of American Tennis, if not of the world. Early in the week Agassi regained his number one ranking when Hewitt lost in the tournament. Roddick added after the match, "I was close in the second set and somehow got to the third, maybe the third set was the one I should not have won." Both Gilbert and Roddick felt the first set was Roddick's best of the year, but this could be all for naught if Agassi won the third set. Despite hitting 12 aces in three consecutive serving games, he stood on the losing end of the set. Roddick played his service game perfectly, but Agassi prevailed. Brad Gilbert looked on anxiously as he watched his new protégé face the man he had coached for 8 years. Gilbert helped bring Agassi's career back from the dead and helped him regain his form. In the first set, Agassi joked that he was worried whether the match would last an hour as he was broken twice, though going into the third set the momentum was in his favor.

Roddick looked shaken early in the third set and was frustrated. And on one changeover, Roddick attacked a trashcan and literally trashed the courts. After destroying the trashcan, Roddick turned his baseball cap around and broke Andre's serve in the second game. The game was back on and now Roddick matched Agassi service game for service game. Each man held serve the rest of the set and now the match was being settled by a second tiebreaker.

Roddick played the tiebreaker aggressively but Agassi took a 6-5 lead and was only one match point away from his fifth straight victory over Roddick. Roddick hit a few tough forehands and tied the match. He then took the lead 7-6 and Agassi served to tie the tiebreaker. Roddick returned Agassi's first serve and prevailed in the ensuing rally when Agassi made his last unforced error—a long forehand.

Roddick exorcised one last demon by beating Agassi. The victory sent a buzz throughout the Tennis world, and now everyone was viewing this victory as a changing of the guard. Certainly, one victory did not spell a new dynasty, and Roddick was still chasing his first major title.

Andy Roddick attracted large crowds during his appearance at Queens. After watching Roddick practice with Goran Ivanisevic, a reporter of the London Guardian wrote, "A much bigger crowd, however, largely consisting of teenage ball girls, has formed alongside the court next door, where Goran Ivanisevic and Andy Roddick are practicing. And it is safe to say the girls, giggling and blushing as they watch, were not there to watch Croatia's favorite Split personality." Typical British understatement. The Guardian reporter viewed Roddick as the All-American kid with "attitude: spiky and bristly and not about to bend to authority." Roddick, the MTV tennis player, who set advertisers heart a flutter!

As for Roddick, the attention meant nothing and he still had to win the finals. Roddick opened the final by nailing two aces and took the opening game. Grosjean nailed a 130 mph serve and took the second game. After five games, each man held their service game but in the sixth game, Roddick got his first break of the game as Grosjean double faulted to give Roddick his fourth game of the set. Roddick took the fifth game easily and Grosjean held Roddick in his next service game. In the final game of the set, Roddick looked sharp at the baseline but looked awkward at the net. Grosjean kept the pressure on, but Roddick took the set with a typical Roddick hard forehand. One set down and one to go for his second title of the season.

In the third game of the second set, Roddick played some deft tennis as he broke Grosjean's service game and held a 2-1 advantage. In the sixth game, Roddick nailed a144 mph serve and in the ninth game, Grosjean was down 5 games to three. Now it became a game of services. Grosjean was quickly down 15-40 as Roddick nailed hard forehands at Grosjean's backhand. Roddick's win did not come as result of a hard forehand or a 140 mph serve though, but a lucky shot, as Roddick's winning match point came with the ball slipping over the top of the net. Roddick won his second title of the year and his first under Brad Gilbert.

Just as Roddick won his preliminary tournament before the French, Roddick won another key tournament before Wimbledon. Roddick said, "I didn't have the easiest draw here but I couldn't be happier right now." Throughout the final, Roddick pressured the Frenchman and his overall performance in the tournament was stellar. Roddick said after the match, "Everything went my way today including match point—it was kind of laughable." Roddick was now ready for Wimbledon and the only thing left was to practice and relax. He won a tournament, foreign tournament at that, and defeated Andre Agassi. Now it was time to take the next step at Wimbledon.

Part Three: Wimbledon

Roddick marched into Wimbledon with confidence. Having taken Queens, and beating Agassi for the first time, Andy was considered a serious dark horse for the title. The first big surprise in Roddick's draw occurred on opening day when Croatian Ivo Karlovic ousted defending champion Lleyton Hewitt in four sets. The draw was now wide open.

Roddick's opening match was a three set victory over David Sanguinetti 6-2, 6-3, 6-3. Roddick's service game was dominant and he never lost a service game. Sanguinetti was back on his heels and Roddick broke him five different times.

The next match was with Greg Rusedski. Roddick beat Rusedski at Queens in a tough three setter, but in the 2002 Wimbledon, it was Rusedski who eliminated Roddick. Rusedski and Roddick shared the record for the fastest serve at 149 mph. And for the British, this was treated as if it was a final. It has been 67 years since a British male won Wimbledon. For the British, their two best hopes were Tim Henman and Greg Rusedski. Henman's history over the past several years was winning five straight matches before losing in the semis at Wimbledon. Rusedski had suffered various injuries but now was ready to challenge. Rusedski had a blazing serve and excellent net game. Roddick was comfortable playing on the baseline but against the 6'4" Rusedski, a more aggressive game was called for.

The winner of this match would be a serious threat for the title. In Rusedski's first match with Andy Waske, there were 50 aces with Greg Rusedski responsible for 31 of those aces. Though Rusedski won in three sets, all three sets were close. Rusedski prevailed in two tiebreakers and the only service break came in the second set as Rusedski broke Waske in the eleventh game.

Rusedski was stoked for this match and every British eye was on him. Roddick marched into Center Court as the betting favorite, but the fans favored their Canadian born citizen. Outside of Court 1, on the large screen TV—thousands of tennis fans streamed over to watch. Rusedski took the opening game and Roddick took the second. Neither man could break the other's serve, and the game headed into a tiebreaker.

Rusedski took the first point and Roddick took the next two. Roddick broke Rusedski's serve and held a 3-2 lead. Roddick and Rusedski traded points and now the score was 4-3. Roddick broke Rusedski's serve and now took a 5-3 lead.

Rusedski took the next point but Roddick closed out the show with a 7-4 tie-breaker win.

The second set was a repeat of the first. Roddick's average serves were quicker, but Rusedski's net game provided Roddick with some trouble. Roddick held his serve and Rusedski held his. Again, the second set ended in a tiebreaker. Roddick nailed the first 6 points and won the tiebreaker easily.

While Roddick was two sets up, Rusedski played Roddick tough and felt that he was still in the game. The third set provided fireworks. Rusedski broke Roddick's serve in the second game and after three games, Rusedski was up three games to zero. Rusedski appeared to be on his way to victory in the third set. Momentum was going his way and Rusedski was slowly crawling back into the match. Roddick was serving in game eight and took a controversial point. Roddick served but Rusedski hit a forehand back. Roddick returned the volley when Rusedski heard someone scream "out." He flailed at the ball and hit the ball out.

The umpire declared it Roddick's point. Rusedski went ballistic for it turned out that the individual yelling out was a fan in the stand. While the chief judge held the option to replay the point, he did not. Rusedski unleashed a few expletives at the judge and threw his racket in disgust. (Later the British tabloid, *the Sun* declared Rusedski's outburst the most dramatic use of the Queen's English uttered by a Canadian.) Roddick won the game and then broke Rusedski in the next game to move within one game of Rusedski. Roddick took the next service game to tie the set. Rusedski, still fuming about the call in the eighth game, was out of synch. He played defensively and quit rushing the net. Looking tired and one step behind, Rusedski lost another service game. Roddick held a 6-5 lead in games, and now it was time to close out the match. Roddick took a 40 to zip lead and now stood one match point away from victory. Rusedski staved off one match point but Roddick blasted one more serve and it was over.

The key to victory was Roddick staying cool while Rusedski was losing his composure. With key plays in the tiebreaker and clutch plays down the stretch run, Roddick won a match against a determined foe on his home court. Rusedski played as good as he ever played for first two sets and a half, but it was Roddick who came away the winner. Now Roddick was headed for the third round against Tommy Robredo, whom he had never lost to.

After the match, when a reporter asked about Roddick's backhand becoming a weapon, Roddick quipped, "It's a weapon now?" He added, "I was hitting my returns pretty well, even though I wasn't breaking a lot." Roddick noted that Rusedski, "had pretty much the same strategy as last year. He was going to make me hit the backhand passing shots."

Tommy Robredo was Roddick's next opponent. Robredo was part of a new generation of Spanish players under the age of 24 who were making their move. An excellent clay player, Robredo was now playing on Roddick's surface. The first set did not resemble the power game of Rusedski vs. Roddick but instead; it resembled a chess game with Robredo returning and volleying from the baseline, forcing long rallies. Robredo was not being intimidated by the Roddick power game. In the crucial twelfth game, Robredo fell behind 0-30 with two weak returns but won the next point with nice serve. The next point was decided in Robredo's favor when he won a 19-stroke rally. Robredo won the game and forced a tiebreaker. This was Roddick's third tiebreak in his last four sets-this includes going back to the Rusedski match. Roddick began the tiebreak with a 131 mph ace. On the second point, Robredo nailed the perfect shot in the corner and Roddick did a split trying to get to the ball. Roddick moved up slowly and then both men split the next four points. The key point happened when Robredo doubled faulted and then Roddick scratched out a 7-5 win in the tiebreak.

Robredo executed graceful shot making skills, forcing Roddick all over the court. Roddick proved to be business like on his service games as both men split the first six games of the set. Robredo had a difficult service game in the seventh game of the set and Roddick took advantage of the Spaniard's momentary lapse to break serve. Roddick now was in the driver's seat, and with his service game crackling, the Spaniard was forced to play the perfect game with no room for error. With the first service break in hand, Roddick served out the next game to take a 5-3 lead. Robredo looked uncomfortable throughout the eighth game as he occasionally yelled in anguish and looked frustrated. He managed to hold his serve in the ninth game but Roddick closed out the show to win the set 6-4.

The third set began with Robredo easily winning the first game, this followed by an easy Roddick service game to counter Robredo's opening salvo. Roddick took his game to a different level as Robredo found himself 0-40 on his second service game. Robredo's last shot hit the net and bounced out. Roddick now had the service break and consolidated his hold, sweeping Robredo four points to zero. On

Robredo's next service game, the Spaniard showed heart as he won the game easily.

Roddick was sailing through his own service game as he had yet to be broken, and at that point, Robredo had no answer for Roddick's serve, which was not just quick but accurate. With the score 5-3, Roddick took Robredo to deuce but the Spaniard managed to win the game and force Roddick to serve for the match. Roddick blistered Robredo with an overpowering serve, and the match ended with a Roddick's forehand smash speeding past Robredo.

Roddick now had gone through three games without losing a set and managed to proceed further than ever in his quest to win at Wimbledon. A new milestone was set, but the next opponent was the dangerous Thai tennis player Srichaphan. Srichaphan was going to be a tough and worthy adversary. Srichaphan had already survived one scare as he was nearly derailed in the second round. He rolled in his third round match though, and now another battle loomed ahead. Roddick stated, "I've had some tough matches so far, so I've had to work to win and I'm probably going to be a quick two-day weekend. It's a new week and a new tournament now. I'll try to start it back up again on Monday."

Monday came and it was now round 16. Andre Agassi was playing the big serving Mark Philippoussis and Roddick was playing the steady Paradorn Srichaphan. Roddick was now in the final 16, this being the farthest he has ever been at Wimbledon. By the end of the day, Roddick would be America's last hope for a crown and the London bookies favorite. Agassi went down in a five set match against Philippoussis as the Australian nailed a Wimbledon record 46 aces. As they say in baseball, good pitching beats good hitting—it could be said that great serving may overcome a good returner.

As for Roddick's match, Srichaphan drew first blood as he took the first game nailing a cross court smash to win the match. Roddick won his first service game that featured a 137 mph serve. The next two games went to the server but in game five, Srichaphan made four unforced errors and Roddick escaped with the first service break. Roddick won the next service game and Srichaphan then switched to a serve and volley strategy as he played more aggressively. In the seventh game, he nailed a perfect drop shot.

Roddick nailed a 140 mph serve as he jumped to a 5-3 lead in the set. The set ended with a love service game as Roddick's torpedo serves finished the first set 6-

4. The second set started with Srichaphan holding his first service game in quick order and he now appeared to hit stride. The next four games had both men holding services and then in the sixth game of the second set, the Thai broke Roddick for the first time and now Srichaphan was in control of the set. The Thai took his next service game and was racing to a 5 game to 2 lead. Roddick staved off match point with an ace in the eighth game but Srichaphan served out and now the match was tied.

Roddick opened the third set with a service victory but Srichaphan tied the set by acing Roddick and then shooting two consecutive winners straight down the line. He stunned Roddick with a beautiful second set. Roddick's game started to shake when he missed two simple backhands but he still held on his serve. While Srichaphan maintained his service game, Roddick was still shaking as he barely hung on to his service game when Srichaphan's forehand went long.

Roddick finally had his service break as he battled Srichaphan in the sixth game. Roddick had three break points but finally prevailed when Srichaphan hit a forehand in the net. Roddick took command and went on to prevail in the third set. Now Roddick had a two sets to one lead.

No longer shaky, Roddick took command. In the third game of the fourth and decisive set, Srichaphan showed the first signs of fatigue as he made one unforced error followed by another. All Roddick had to do was to hold serve and the Thai had to force a Roddick break, something that he had only done once in the match. While Roddick held his serve, Srichaphan once again proved unsteady on his service game, and Roddick was just two games away from the match and the quarterfinals. Roddick took a five game to one lead as he served out the sixth game with ease. Srichaphan snapped back to win the seventh game but Roddick served his out his last game and the match was over. Roddick looked impressive once again, and through four matches, lost only one set. Now he was three-matches away from his first major.

Roddick had yet to lose a match since coming to England and part of that appeared to be the result of changing coaches. Roddick had been under the tutelage of Tarik Benhabiles for the past three years, and though Tarik managed to turn Roddick into a top ten player, Roddick's defeat at the French Open ended the relationship. Roddick turned to Brad Gilbert, Andre Agassi's former coach and the man who directed Agassi's rise back to the top. Gilbert's job was to get Roddick to the top as he did Agassi, and as a result, Roddick appeared to be a different player after the coaching change. While the Australian Open showed Roddick's guts, Wimbledon was starting to look like Roddick's coming out party. Roddick was playing with more confidence and executing a more patient game. Roddick proved adept at hiding his weaknesses and appeared cooler under pressure. And now with the top two seeds out, this was his first big opportunity to win a major. The next man up was the unseeded Jonas Bjorkman.

After the match and the loss of Agassi, the bookies' choice to win Wimbledon became Roddick. When asked about the possibility, Roddick responded, "Brad's philosophy is if you want to win a Grand Slam, you've got to win seven matches. You've got to knock people down as they come, regardless, anytime, you've got to win seven matches. That's kind of the approach that I've taken. Win three sets every other day, do that seven times." Roddick added that the unseeded Jonas Bjorkman was his most serious threat since "he's the guy that I play next." Roddick was also asked about his relationship with his previous coach Tarik Benhabiles, Roddick replied, "I got an e-mail from Tarik this morning. He said, 'good job. Keep going. Try to take it all the way.' We have plans to go to dinner when I get back. My friendship with Tarik will never be gone."

Wimbledon finally was hit with English rain as the Men's quarterfinals were wiped out. Henman-Grosjean and the Phillppoussis—Popp matches could not be completed, and the Federer match with Schalken along with Roddick-Bjorkman were canceled. The next day, the Roddick match was delayed nearly 2 hours, and in the first four games, Roddick appeared shaky. Bjorkman nailed four straight points to open the match including two aces, and after Roddick broke Bjorkman's serve in the third game, he promptly lost it with the set now tied 2-2.

In the fifth game, Bjorkman was on his way to an easy victory with a 40-love lead. Roddick managed to get the game back to deuce and finally converted on his third break point when Bjorkman's return went into the net. Now Roddick needed to convert on his service game. This he did as he served out with authority. Now Roddick took control of the set. Bjorkman stayed in the set with a victory in the seventh game and Roddick, setting a pattern, easily took a service game. Roddick would never lose another service game in the match. While Bjorkman defended his service game Roddick served out the set, and was now one set down and only two to go.

In the second set, Roddick took control as his power serves wore down the gallant Swede. Roddick broke Bjorkman's service game to open the set and breezed to an easy second game victory with monster serves. Bjorkman with a crafty serve and volley game attempted to keep the Roddick express from leaving, but Roddick took the next three games including another service break. Bjorkman saved a service game though Roddick served out the set to prevail 6-2.

It was two sets down and one to go for Roddick's first semifinal appearance at Wimbledon. Despite being down two sets to nothing, Bjorkman was not quite ready to surrender. After being down 2 games, Bjorkman held on to his service game in the third game and stayed in the match. A little drama appeared as Bjorkman seemed to temporarily derail the Roddick express, but in the fifth game Roddick sealed the game with a forehand return across court, forcing Bjorkman to lose his fifth service game of the match. Bjorkman showed the first signs of despair as Roddick took a service love game. Roddick was playing the perfect game and Bjorkman had to break Roddick to have a chance.

Roddick appeared to coast in the seventh game, and the results were no longer in doubt. Roddick's power was the difference, and now he was two-matches from his first major. The next opponent was the Swiss star Roger Federer. Federer was seeded one ahead of Roddick, and like Roddick, Federer was playing at his best. While Roddick garnered the headlines, Federer was just under the radar screen. Like Roddick though, he was looking for his first major. A talented player with all the shots, Federer would be Roddick's sternest test since Roddick had lost his previous three matches against the young Swiss. Roddick, who beat Agassi at Queens for the first time, must now beat Federer for the first time.

Roger Federer, like Roddick, has been suffering from the big P—Potential. A year older than Roddick, Federer gave an indication of his potential when he eliminated Pete Sampras in his previous Wimbledon but for most part he had not yet been a factor in the majors. Sampras predicted before Wimbledon that Federer would prevail and considered Federer's game to be the best all around. It was Roddick's big serve vs. Federer's all around game.

Roddick, the bookies' favorite, was shooting his scorching serve, which caused Federer discomfort in the early part of the game. Federer's own first serves were accurate and enabled him to level the playing field. As the first set progressed, Federer started pressuring Roddick, and though Roddick held on to his serve in the set, so did Federer. The first set showed the unflappable and relaxed style of Federer contrasted to the more aggressive American. The first set went to a tie-break.

The tiebreak seesawed between the two. Federer took a 4-2 lead and was ready to put it away when a simple volley went awry. Roddick took the next three point and then Federer tied it up. Roddick came within a set point as he drilled a forehand. Roddick nailed his next forehand in the net and then Federer broke Roddick's serve. Now it was Federer who was one point away from set point. Federer served out the tiebreak and took a one set up.

Federer opened the set up by getting his first serve in, but Federer started to struggle with his serve giving Roddick a chance to break Federer's service game. Instead, Federer saved his service game and then it was Roddick who would lose service game and fall behind the Swiss 2 games to 0 early in the set.

Federer took his next service game, and after five games seemed in control. In the seventh game, Roddick appeared to lose his cool as he protested a call from the umpire. Trying to inspire himself, Roddick acted animated but Federer still won the game and now was one game from taking a two set to zero lead.

Serving in game eight, Roddick looked more fired up as he took the game easily; but at this point, he had only four aces. This statistic only showed Federer's control of the game. Federer seized the second set and now was one set away from his first major.

Roddick opened up the crucial third set with an easy service game, but in the second game Federer lost only one point to the more aggressive Roddick and appeared cool under fire.

By the fifth game, Roddick showed the first signs of frustration as Federer broke Roddick for the second time in the match. By this point, Federer was making every shot in the book, and after serving out the sixth game was just two games away from winning the match. In the seventh game, Roddick served out four straight points but Federer showed his superiority on this day as he threw an ace to move one game closer. Roddick now had to hold his service game and break Federer, something that he had not done all game.

At 30-30, Federer smacked a forehand against the static Roddick. Roddick saved the game with a desperation point. Federer lured Roddick to the net and zipped a forehand shot right past him. Roddick tried to counterattack but his forehand went out. Federer won the match of the young gunslingers.

After the match, Roddick said, "All credit to him, he played one match. As far as talent goes, I don't know if there's anyone there more talented," Roddick said, "He's a great athlete, he is so quick out there. There's not much he doesn't have."

Federer was ecstatic and told reporters, "It's incredible. Right now it's tough to understand what has been happening. I just played an incredible match. This is my favorite tournament. It's a dream."

Tennis week Brad Falkner wrote of Federer, "Tennis isn't easy, but Federer can make it look that way. Federer's vast variety of shots and ability to play offensive tennis from virtually any position on the court were too much for Roddick to overcome." At this point in their careers, Federer's overall skill was enough to keep Roddick from using his big service game and establishing a rhythm.

Wimbledon was almost Roddick's coming out party but was instead the second time that Roddick lost in the semis in a major. After winning ten straight matches on grass, Roddick lost for the first time since playing in England. What was apparent though, was that Roddick's relationship with his new coach started out on the right foot.

Part Four: Queuing in Wimbledon

(Beth Donelson joined members of the Roddick'n'Roll website for several days. For many in Wimbledon, queuing is a Wimbledon tradition. Queuing is the British way of waiting in line for tickets and for many, queuing begins with an overnight stay in tents along the road. Beth, along with many Roddick'n'Rollers, camped out the night before to buy tickets for center court to catch Andy's first match on Court one. These are her experiences.)

There is nothing like visiting Wimbledon. I met with members of the Roddick'n' Rollers website. Terms needed to know include: going for a wee dander"....What's in tooting?....queuing in the rain....Pimms and strawberries and cream on Henman hill....Security risk for Mr. Gambill....Do horses eat potatoes?....Cheering against the tide.

I did some more exploring around London after we arrived and then headed back to the hotel to get ready to meet up with Anne, Rachael, Caz and her two friends Jeff and Nicola as well as Tatjana. Tatjana was the first to arrive. It's a good thing she didn't come any sooner because I had just finished my shower. I felt that for an event with as much prestige as Wimbledon I should be clean. Not to mention it wouldn't be until Monday night before I would be able to shower again. Tatjana and I talked a bit, and it seems that she and her friends had a little party upon her arrival. As we were catching up, everyone else came at the same time. So how convenient! We did all the introductions, hugged each other and then went to business. We decided to get our dinner to take with us to the queue, so we put our luggage in our room and headed in search of food. After looking at our options we decided on just going to the grocer and buying meat and cheese for sandwiches. We made our purchases, retrieved our luggage and headed to Southfield to join the queue.

It was about 6:30pm when we got there. There was a very nice old man at the end of the queue to welcome us. When you queue, they give you a card with a number as proof that you did in fact queue all night and approximately where you are in the line. It's very good to keep hold of it because you won't like the answer if you lose it. (Luckily, none of us got to hear that answer but Caz did try to see what would happen Tuesday. So, with our queue cards in hand and a pretty good position in line, we were set.) Right across the street from where we were, there were people selling adult Wimbledon t-shirts. Not those kinds of adult t-shirts! We went to work on our tents. Jeff and Nicola brought a tent and

Rachael had brought a tent that she borrowed from a friend. Now Jeff and Nicola had no trouble with their tent, but Rachael's was another story, and Anne and Caz were no help, no help whatsoever. They just stood there and laughed and with good reason! At one point we had a teepee, instead of a tent. Rachael was forced to call her friend and yell at her "You liar, you said this was going to be easy!"

About a half an hour later, we finally got the tent up, even though it was a bit lopsided. We didn't have a lot of room for our two tents. We had to make due with the cramped space, enjoyed our dinner and talked about the upcoming matches. While the rest of us were struggling with the tents, Anne and Caz noticed that one of the buses was going to Tooting. Of course, with great curiosity we wondered what there was to do in Tooting. It also inspired the two to break out in laughter.

Tennis is an international sport and the Roddick'n'Rollers on this trip included both English and Irish visitors as well as American fans. The various Roddick websites had visitors from Singapore, Ireland, England, France, the United States and the rest of the world. Roddick is more known in England than let's say, Barry Bonds or Brett Favre. Most Tennis stars have followings that stretch across national lines and Tennis fans do not care that much for national designations.

Around 8 or something like that Anne had to report to her job cleaning toilets in Wimbledon, so she left us to do that. The rest of us got tired of being cramped so we moved to the street. The people in front of us and behind us in the queue had their cars, which left us a perfect place to sit and chat. Of course it also meant that every time they unlocked their cars, their headlights blinded us. The best thing about this trip is all the slang used. The topper of them all was when Jeff decided to go for a walk or as he put it "a wee dander." This was new to all of us non-Irish types. I think we all used that expression hundreds of times in the next couple of days. For those who don't know what a dander is, a dander is a short walk with no real destination. My sister Kat and I later found out in our trip to Scotland, they might use the word gander, in the place of dander but it's the same thing. Jeff went on his wee dander and the rest of us stayed. We kind of watched the official cars go by to see if we could recognize any players. We recognized Martin Verkerk in one of the cars and that caused a stir among the group!

Now, it pretty much drizzled off and on throughout the night but it wasn't until around midnight that it started to come down hard enough to really bother us and force us into our tents. Caz, Jeff and Nicola stayed in one and Rachael, Tat-jana, Kat and I slept in the other. It was pretty cramped to say the least. It was hard to sleep with the rain and when it stopped raining we could hear singing, buses and cars. And did I mention it was cramped and we were sleeping on the hard pavement? Not so pleasant. The various paperboys started to make the rounds around 5:30am, which was just too early. Who reads the newspaper at 5:30 in the morning anyway? An hour later, the stewards woke us, telling us that we had to be ready to move just after seven. Ugh. So, in the rain, we took down our tents and huddled together. It stopped raining about two hours later and it was pretty steaming for the rest of the day.

Halfway, through the queue we had to split up. Most of us had luggage so we went into an area where you could leave your tents and other luggage. The rest stayed with the queue. Well, it was taking them too long with the left luggage so, the line split again and we went on to meet the rest on the line to get our bracelets for our tickets. Kat got Centre seats to see Guga, (Kat's favorite player), Jeff got court two to see Venus losing he hoped, (Jeff is not a Venus Williams fan) and Nicola just got grounds passes and the rest of us got court one to see Andy! Nice yellow bracelets! We got them and other freebies. Returned to Left Luggage and dropped off our luggage then went back in line and waited for the gates to open to buy our tickets. After sleeping on the pavement, standing in the rain, waiting in line, tolerating bag searches, we finally purchased our tickets in the second row behind the players. It was sweet. We had to wait in a holding area until the rest of the place was open, but it gave us a chance to visit the ladies room and get some food. Choose seats and that is what queuing is all about.

We made a beeline to the practice courts when they opened the gates. I don't remember who all was practicing, but we noticed a young player talking with a certain coach who was wearing a Metallica Gilligan hat. Yep it was Andy. We saw him practice for a bit and took some pictures but it was really crowded. Everyone wanted to see him, so we left and left the masses to it. We then took a wee dander around the facility. Kinda looking for the Kid Zone area. We were going to have a crappiest serve contest but when we got there, there were little kids about nine and ten who were hitting serves over 70 mph. (At many baseball stadiums, there are areas where you can measure how fast your fastball is and at Wimbledon, you can see how fast your serve is. Or isn't.) Well, in the interest of not completely humiliating ourselves, we decided to come back later when there were fewer people. We never did get back there. Lucky for me, but I do know I would have won easily for I have a pathetic serve.

Play started at noon on all the outside courts. And there was a very interesting match out on court six. Rafi vs. SuperMario! So, we negotiated our ways through the maze of courts and masses of people looking for court 6. Believing it was easy to find, we found it's a bit out of the way from the other courts. People had already gathered and the seats were taken. There was a patch of grass to sit on so we found space for the five of us: Tatjana, Anne, Caz, Rachael and I. We should have known that the grass would be wet because it did rain that morning, so we all had ended up with wet behinds. For our first match at Wimbledon, I think it was a very good match to start with. From the beginning Rafi was in control. He was up a break when we left to see Andy. He's definitely going places but before he does, he needs to break his habit of picking his wedgies before every serve. Sorry to be so vulgar, but seriously, every time he served, he adjusted himself in that manner. Someone needs to buy that boy bigger undies before his matches start getting aired on TV. That's all that needs to be said on that subject. Like I said, we left with Rafi up a break in the first and headed for court 1. We didn't want to miss a second of Andy's match so we got there early. Second row, right behind the players and more specifically right behind Andy!!!

Andy came out all in white with orange trimmings on his clothes. No visor. I still think it's unfair that Andy is not allowed to wear the visor but Brad gets to wear his stupid Metallica hat. (Gilbert had Roddick give up his visor because it was not intimidating enough but it caused a stir among Roddick's fans that just loved the visor. The days of the visor are over. Brad Gilbert told my sister that visors are weak and for women's doubles.) It was Andy's match to win. He just dominated David Sanguinetti the entire match. I think Andy had one break point against him in the whole match. It was a quick match. Secretly, I wished it had gone longer but I was happy that Andy went through it with little drama. After the match, we met up with another Roddick fan, Lucy on Henman Hill (located outside Court one and in front of the big screen TV. The hill is named for British favorite Tennis player, Tim Henman.) On the Screen, they were showing Hewitt losing. When it happened, a wave of shock came over everyone on the hill. My sister Kat had front row seats for that match and she said that Llegs was just outplayed by Ivo and from what we saw, that was definitely true. Poor Llegs. The man was almost in tears as he left the court.

Lucy, Tatjana and I stayed around the Hill and talked and waited to see if Andy would walk by. The rest of the girls went to check out the practice courts again to see who was there. For people watching, Henman Hill was the place to be. While we didn't see Andy walk by, we saw tons of players walk by on their way to and from the practice courts. Most of them we could only tell were players because of the rackets, a big tip-off. I still say that players should be given name tags, so we can identify them.

When the other girls returned, we had lunch. I was shocked to find Pizza and hamburgers and noodles to eat at Wimbledon. I was thinking it would be more like Roland Garros and they would just have sandwiches. I'm an American, so this didn't bother me. I mean I live in the land of hot dogs and nacho cheese. That's what we eat at sporting events. I think I had Pizza that day. I'm still a bit confused why they called pepperoni pizza, Mexican pizza. Wouldn't Mexican be closer to taco pizza? Oh well. After lunch, we went to watch more matches. We bounced from one court to another.

We made plans to meet at Southfields at 7:30am to queue for grounds passes. If we knew that Anne's train was going to be late we could have all slept in for an extra hour, well maybe not Anne. (Since Roddick was not scheduled to play, it did not matter whether we received tickets.) Jeff and Nicola went on ahead while Caz and I waited for Anne. Rachael unfortunately couldn't come and Tatjana came with her friends and we saw her later. One of the best things about queuing is the freebies you get in line. We received sunscreen, Listerine strips, stickers, and a whole bunch of other stuff. So, as we waited in the line, we had our breakfast of ice cream, read our newspapers and had an all Disney sing-a-long.

Like on Monday, as soon as we got in, we went straight for the practice courts. Younes was practicing and so was "Our Tim". (The Brits are very possessive about their players. When you read the tabloid, Henman is referred to as "Our Tim.") You can imagine how crazy it was around that court. So, we left for court 3 to see Coria and Tiny, aka Olivier Rochus. It was a very popular court, so we had to split up. Caz and Nicola sat together and I sat with Anne but she was very nervous. We were sitting next to Belgian fans so every time she yelled out "Go Guillermo!!!" They yelled out to Tiny! Oh, I forgot. I can't believe I forgot this. On Monday, We saw Coria practicing, so of course we had to watch. He was just finishing up when we got there. Anne got very bashful, and after he left we had a moment of indecision if we should go after him or not. (Not only is Anne a big fan of Roddick's but also loves to watch Coria.) Well, we did. He stopped to take a look at the results monitor and was by himself. We tried to get Anne to go up to him. It was the perfect opportunity because he was alone and no one was around. Well, she all of a sudden became bashful so Caz and I walked up to him. His back was to us, so in my most polite and respectful voice said, "Guillermo, can I take a photo?" And he said yes, I kinda had him pose for me. Caz took one as well, we said, "thank you," and he left. (Tennis players are very assessable to the public.)

Back to the match, which was not going Coria's way. Let's just say, grass does not agree with him. I have never seen someone spend so much time on the grass and when he wasn't falling on the grass he was kicking it and hitting it with his racket. Poor Guy. Tiny won pretty easily. The funny thing was that Mark Philippoussis was playing three courts down and he still looked like a Giant compared to Oli and Coria.

After the match, we had to cheer up a disappointed Anne and alcohol was always good for that. And we had some Pimms and strawberries and cream. So very posh of us. (Strawberry Cream is what makes the Wimbledon experience complete and Pimms is an English alcoholic cocktail.) As we were enjoying our refreshments, Caz or Nicola noticed that Jan Mike (Jan Michael Gambill, one of the sexier players on the circuit.) was walking by, and out of nowhere I yell out to Jan Mike to wait! I still can't believe he stopped. I was rummaging through my bag, looking for Fee's letter. (Fee, whose real name is Fiona, is a big Gambill fan and met Gambill, while working at a West Coast tournament. Fee is also a big Roddick fan and it could easily be said that Fee is a tennis fan period for she follows the Tennis scene closely. Fee told me that if I saw Gambill, to pass on this letter.) I couldn't find it and knowing that Jan Mike was waiting for me, I walked over to him. Still looking. I basically had to get on the ground and start taking things out of my bag like my clothes for tomorrow (so embarrassing) and unbeknownst to me, a security guard was behind me. I guess he thought I was a security risk or something. Anyway, I was now in full search of Fee's letter and I told Jan Mike, thanks for waiting, that I had a letter for him from Fiona Simon, his response, "Oh, Cool!" So, articulate that man is. He then said, "When you talk to her, let her know I like her website." I said, "Oh so you've seen it?" Jan Mike: "Yes" I responded, "Cool." (Fee also runs a website devoted to Jan Michael. She also writes for other Tennis website and is knowledgeable about the game. She also has many friends in the Tennis world) By that time I finally found it. It was at the bottom of my bag, all wrinkled and a little torn. I couldn't believe I'm giving this crinkled piece of paper to Jan Mike! I apologized for it being all torn and wrinkled and he was like "no problem and thanks" and was on his way. I went back to the ladies on the hill, who were laughing at me, and they told me about the guard.

We headed back to the practice courts and passed Andy doing an autograph session. We decided to skip that queue. No one of real interest was practicing except for a Guga wannabe that everyone thought was Guga but not me. I was not fooled. We saw the real Guga later. We then headed over to see some of Blakes' match. It was court five and standing room only. We stayed long enough to get our photos of James and then set out for a court in the shade. We found one with a Canadian player whose name I can't remember and Felix Mantilla. It wasn't the most exciting match but we managed to sit in the shade for a bit so that was nice. We watched a few more matches, went back to the practice courts and by this time it was coming up on six so we called Lucy to see when we should queue for the next day. Andy was preparing to meet Greg Rusedski.

Anne called Lucy to ask where she was so we could all meet up and queue together. We were at Gate 1 and Lucy said she would be right there. Well, the All England Club is a big Club and Lucy went out Gate four instead of one. She called Anne back, said where she was and that she was getting in the Wimbledon queue instead of the Southfield. We weren't exactly sure where that was but we decided to get our bags from left luggage before looking for the other queue. Of course, we didn't mention this to Lucy who was getting a bit worried where we were. When we found Lucy, she and Tatjana had gotten their queue cards, so it was too late to join them but she said that Rachael was in line already and we should find her. Off we went to find Rachael. She was five people behind Lucy and she caught up to us. We asked the Steward if it was ok if we cut in line to join her. The queue wasn't that long behind her so it was ok. Much to the relief of all of us, Rachael had the tent and it would have sucked for her to queue alone. The Stewards came around and gave us our queue cards, so we were all set for the night.

At this point, Caz and Nicola went for a wee dander to Wimbledon village and I went to go chat with Lucy, who was by herself because Tatjana had left to get refreshments for the evenings activities. Lu and I talked for a bit, mostly about Andy's match against Greg the next day. Anyway, our duel conversation became a quartet.

I've already mentioned all the great freebies you get when you queue but neglected all the restaurants that are willing to deliver directly to you in line. Of course, I'm sure they make much from queuers that don't want to leave the line. So, Caz, Anne, Rachael and I went through all the menus that had been given us, debating on what we wanted and what was the cheapest. We finally agreed on the

"Wimbledon Feast", a large pizza, potato skins, garlic bread and bottle of soda, all for a modest £12.99. Ok, I think that's modest. I never did fully understand the whole conversion rate, except for the fact that I was spending more with everything I buy. (The American dollar was down compared to the pound and this made it more expensive to convert.) Rachael ordered the meal and then we had the whole ordeal of telling them where we were in line, and then they said, "It'll be about 30 minutes, Mrs. Rachael." So polite, the English. We all had a good laugh about that but I think it took more then 30 minutes for the meal and maybe it felt like forever because we were starving. When it finally did come, we all dove in. We ate everything except for one potato skin.

The newspaper people (so PC of me) came again around 5:30am. Again I ask, who needs to have a newspaper that early in the morning? Anyway, we all ignored them for about 30 minutes to an hour but the rustling of the people around us forced us to get up for real. So, we went through the whole routine of taking down the tent and getting our selves prepared for the days events. The really nice Australian couple that was behind us offered to take our photos for us. They were queuing veterans. This was their twelfth year. They were really cool, especially since they were rooting for Andy to beat Greg. Roddick even has fans in Australia. Over the speakers, they were playing the BBC/Wimbledon Radio. Of course, it was biased in favor of Rusedski. This match was given the Royal treatment and treated as if it was a heavyweight fight. Every pub in England had this match. One of the so-called experts said that he didn't think Andy was as improved as people were saying. Whatever! Of course he also said that Andy had beaten Greg in straight sets at Queens (Andy won two of the three sets in a close match.) and that Nadal was16!(Nadal was 17.)

We tried to get a hold of Lucy and Tatjana, to see if they could wait for us to buy their tickets so we could all sit together but we were never successful. Oh well. As we got closer and closer to the gate it felt like forever to get through. At one point we saw Kat go through to buy her court 1 tickets. She was like way behind us, so how did she manage to beat us! Well we finally got in. Our seats were right behind the players in the second row and let's just say we were stoked!

First order of business was to change into our shirts once we got inside of the gates. So, we did that and looked absolutely fantabulous if I do say so myself. We then found Kat who was waiting in the queue to be let into the rest of the park. She was also looking fantabulous in her Roddick'n'Roll/Margaux's Miracle shirt.

When we got there, it was standing room only and who knew that it would be such a popular court. The players came out. Mardy was pushing the all white rule with his red headband. Jan Mike was still wearing his warm-up pants and when he took them off, Rach announced to everyone "Jan Mike is taking his trousers off!" It got a good laugh from everyone around us. The guy in front of us, who was enjoying a glass of champagne said "Wait until he takes his shirt off!" We watched for a few games but decided that since we had spent the money for Centre court tickets that we should use them and went off to see Roger. We were all expecting him to lose and for most of the first set he didn't disappoint but when Koubek served for it, Rogi (Roger Federer, the eventual Wimbledon champion) woke up. After the first set, we decided to go get something for lunch. While we were eating on the hill, it started to drizzle a little bit but not enough to stop play, and on the big screen they showed the guys that were sitting in front of us.

The rain stopped, so we bought our Pimms and went back to Centre court. When the play was stopped, Roger was up 5-1 and he played flawless tennis. Even though we were so sure he was going to lose, at least we could say that we saw the Champion Play at least once while we were there. Venus was next and she was quite impressive. Like her sister, she definitely had a demanding presence on the court. After the first set, we went to prepare ourselves for Andy. Kat and I (it was mostly Kat's idea but I take partial credit) bought our British fans American style band-aids as a thank you gift for bringing tents and sleeping bags and stuff like that. Our gifts from America! Well, we thought it would be a fab idea to wear them on our faces a la Nelly but they were too big. So, we had to improvise. I put two on my Wimbly hat and the others put them on their wrist so it would be visible when they pumped their fists. After we were all beautiful for cheering on Andy, we went back to see that Venus was still in control. She went on to win easily.

Now, with Roger and Venus over, the nerves started to creep in. From where we were seated, we could see the players when they got on the court. I think we lost it when we saw Andy. The tension was already high in that court. Like Caz said after the match, it was like a Davis Cup Match with Andy playing for the away country. It definitely made things exciting. Now from the first game, I knew Andy was going to win. He had a break point opportunity on Greg's serve. I just knew he was going to win. The British crowd was definitely with Greg for some odd reason. He's Canadian for goodness sake! But the one good thing about Americans is that as a people we are loud! And we make sure we were heard no matter where we went. We taught our European counterparts how to make noise.

Halfway, through the second set, a group of people followed our lead and starting cheering "Andy Andy Andy Oi oi oi!" There was one American girl behind us who was confused why we were using that one because it was an "Australian cheer" but we told her we co-opted it as our own and no one has ever accused cheerleaders of being original. We had a lot of American students around us who joined with us in our cheers.

Andy totally dominated the second set tiebreak and had a few break points in the first game of the third but Greg held on. Andy played a sloppy service game to lose his serve. At 5-2 and Andy serving to stay in the third set, the crowd started to get into it. The now famous Greg outburst stunned the crowd in the eighth game and from that point on Andy just took over the game. (One British tabloid complimented Rusedski for his innovative use of the Queen's English.) Let's just say, we were all on cloud nine after the match. Andy threw a ball in Lucy's direction but the girls in front of her grabbed it. After Andy left triumphantly, they announced that Kim Clijsters match would be played next, so I left the girls there and went to find my family on the hill.

Anne, Caz and I said good-bye to Rach, who had to catch her train home. It was so sad saying good-bye to her because she was so cool and I knew I would have to say good-bye to Anne and Caz soon too. We milled around a bit more, caught up with Lucy, her mom Judith and Judith's friend Polly and talked about Andy's match. Everyone was excited about Andy's victory. We had been talking about meeting at Wimbledon and queuing for over a year and then it was all over. It went by too quickly. We met up with Kat and had to climb up the hill towards Wimbledon Village to get her left luggage, then had to get Anne and Caz's left luggage. Caz had this brilliant idea of getting a taxi to Southfields. Why walk, when we can drive! The adventure was over and we went our separate ways.

4

The Hard Court Season to the US Open

Part One: World Team Tennis: First Taste of Hard Court.

After Wimbledon, it was back to the States and the hard court season. Like Grass, Hard Courts suited the Roddick power game and Roddick was becoming more comfortable with Brad Gilbert, his new coach.

After Wimbledon, for the most part, the ATP tour cannot wait to get off the grass. Of the three tournaments that follow Wimbledon, only one of them is on grass and the other two are on clay, that's right, clay, the same surface that the players were on before Wimbledon. Basically, the only players that played that week were all the clay-court specialists that have miraculously recovered from the injuries that left them out of the third Grand Slam of the year and all the journey men that play week in and week out no matter what the surface is. Roddick obviously didn't fit in either one of those categories. He only took a week off after his semifinal loss to Roger Federer before returning to the court. Not to play a tournament but instead relax and have fun in the environment of World Team Tennis. Roddick in his third season for St. Louis Aces played two matches for the team, and used these matches just to take a breather from the tour.

World Team Tennis was founded by tennis legend Billie Jean King in 1974, as a way to make tennis more accessible to the average fans. It's a mixed event that features a set of men's singles, women's singles, both men's and women's doubles and mixed doubles. At the end the number of games is added together and whichever team has the most games wins the match. Confused yet? Well, it has had many tennis fans scratching their heads for years but year after year big name players have signed up to play. Along with Roddick, other marquee players were Andre Agassi, John McEnroe, Anna Kournikova, James Blake and Lindsay Davenport. None of them play the whole season, Roddick played in two matches for the Aces, once in Schenectady, New York, and one home game in St. Louis. One can only imagine what excitement Roddick brought to a format that brought out the showman in Roddick, when he was already known as one of the most exciting players of the tour. Kathleen Nelson of the St. Louis Post-Dispatch said recently of Andy's popularity among fans. "He has become popular for his break dancing, his 149 mph serve and his ability to balance a good time with fierce competitiveness." In one of his matches, Andy supposedly hit a 150 mph serve and then proceeded to do a little dance with the ball boys. According to Rebecca, a fan that attended Roddick's first match against the New York Buzz, reported that some male fans were heckling Roddick, Roddick yelled back "next round is on me, boys". For Tennis fans in Missouri, this was the opportunity to see one of the game's best for the weekend.

Andy flew into Saint Louis on July 12th to team with Nicole Arendt, John Laffnie de Jager, Amir Hadad and Julia Vakulenko. Roddick was the star attraction and did not disappoint as he nailed a 150 mph strike against the New York Buzz.

Andy won his single but Roddick and Arendt lost their mixed doubles 5-4 with the tiebreaker going 7-4. The match opened with a loss in the men's doubles, and the Buzz took the match by the score of 22-15.

The next night, the Aces went up against the Kansas City Explorers. Just as they did the night before, the mixed doubles team of Arendt and Roddick fell short and just as the night before, Roddick won his single. The team of Roddick and De Jager won their doubles match and the Aces nipped the Explorers 19-18 with Roddick doing his duty for WTT.

World Team Tennis didn't just allow Andy to relax and have fun on the court but gave him a chance to interact with his fans as well. He did numerous signings while he was on site. After his match in St. Louis, Andy spent some time with fans, including Stef, from Kansas City, who were staying at the same hotel as he was. After being told of a certain photo contest, Andy came up with the perfect pose. With the help of Stef and her friends, they assisted Andy in a handstand and held him up long enough for Stef's mom to take a picture. While the competition of WTT isn't exactly ideal for gearing up for the summer hard court season and the US Open at the end of August, it is a nice diversion from the every day grind of the ATP tour.

The next match was the RCA Championships in Indianapolis.

Part Two: Roddick at Indy

Roddick entered the Indianapolis RCA tournament as the number one seed with his first match a tough meeting against the tricky Frenchman Cyril Saulnier. As Roddick said after the match, Saulnier's strategy was to "just poke it back." Roddick felt frustrated the entire match, never getting a handle on his opponent, as the closeness of the score would indicate. The first set went to Saulnier on a tiebreaker, which Saulnier won 7-5. After Roddick served to get within one point, Saulnier served out the tiebreaker to preserve the set and take a one set lead.

After the match, Roddick said, "It's almost like the better shots I'd hit, the better shots he'd come up with." Roddick added, "He was serving well. He was hitting his spots. I think he played a pretty smart match." Roddick felt the match had a surreal feel to it as he explained, "It was frustrating. I felt I was getting the better end of him, and I'd be down a set and a break."

In the second set, Roddick fell behind 3 games to one and was on the verge of being the first number one seed in nearly a decade to lose in the first round. Roddick broke Saulnier's serve twice and swept the last five games. In the third set, both men played nip and tuck tennis as they each negated the other's strength. Just as in the first set, both men held serve and, once again, the set was decided by a tiebreaker. Roddick now was facing elimination in the first round of a tournament in which he was the favored player. On hard court no less, which played to Roddick's power game.

The final tiebreak was 3-3 before Roddick zipped off four of the last five points to prevail 7-4. Saulnier's last shot sailed long past the line and allowed Roddick to escape with the win. Game, Set, Match.

Roddick finished the match with 17 aces though Saulnier produced 13 of his own.

If Roddick's match with Saulnier was a nail biter, his match with Gregory Carraz was a quick affair, lasting 60 minutes. Roddick marched into the quarterfinals as he made quick work of Carraz 6-3, 6-4.

Carraz's opening game included three double faults in the opening game and as Roddick said, "I'm not sure if he was nervous in that game, but those three doubles set the tone." Roddick's rushes to the net unnerved Carraz and while Roddick's service game was inconsistent, he was faced with only one break point the entire match. From the opening serve, Roddick controlled the match.

After the match, Roddick said, "My game felt a lot cleaner tonight. After a month on grass, I hadn't hit a ball above my shoulders for a long time." Of course,

Roddick was asked the obligatory question about when he was taking over Sampras's spot in American Tennis and he answered, "I can't help the hype around me. But maybe now with the semi-finals in Australia and Wimbledon, maybe they know I'm trying, I'm trying to take it to the next level."

On his service game, Roddick commented, "I thought I could have put a lot more first serves in tonight." He added that he would have to work on his serve as he moved further in the tournament.

Meanwhile, while Roddick was playing in Indianapolis, other former tennis greats, John McEnroe and Martina Navratilova were leading a movement to de-emphasize the power game of tennis. Their proposal included reducing the size of racket heads, therefore limiting the area of the "sweet spot." Of this movement, Roddick stated, "People talk about power, power, power, but there's still more to our game."

Roddick, like Sampras before him, depended upon the power game and merely retorted that his game was the result of better equipment and training. Roddick said, "I don't see the point of all the talk now—we are going to get faster because it's the nature of sports to find people improving." Roddick added, "I've still got 10 years ahead of me and I've broken the [serving record] already."

In just under one hour, Roddick dismantled Belgian Xavier Malisse 6-4, 6-1. Roddick's game was as clean as it was dominating with twenty-eight winners scored against the Belgian. In the second set, Malisse took a medical time out down four games to one but this failed to stop the onslaught The only hope that Malisse had of winning the match came as he took the first two points of the second set. After that, Roddick took over. He took the first game and while Malisse held serve in the second game, that was all for the Belgian. For the rest of the set, Malisse only managed to score 10 points over the next five games. With Malisse out of the way, Roddick marched into the semi-finals.

In his post match interview, Roddick said, "Anytime you reach the semis at your first event after switching surfaces, it's welcome." Roddick added, "Because of the way I was serving in the first set, I felt okay, although in the last set and a half, I really got some momentum going."

Roddick was facing the experienced Dutch player Sjeng Schalken, whose strength was in his return and baseline game. Schalken broke in the third game and took an early 2-1 lead. Roddick negated Schalken's advantage in the fourth game when he claimed Schalken's serve. Then in the sixth game, Roddick once again overcame Schalken's serves to take control of the first set 6-2. Roddick took the last four games.

The second set opened with Roddick serving to capture the first game and then he stole another service game from Schalken to take a 2-zip lead. From this point, he sauntered home to the finals. Roddick had only five aces but he won 18 of the 21 first-serve points. In the second set, Roddick won the last three games after Schalken defended his serve in the fifth game.

Later, Roddick told reporters, "I got sloppy when I was broken in the first set, but I knew I would have chances to break back." Roddick complained about his service games when he told reporters, "I didn't serve very well today. I realized that early on but concentrated on just getting a high percentage and working on the second shot." When asked about his coach's contribution, he said, "Maybe that's where Brad has helped a bit…he tells me there's more than one way to win or lose a tennis match."

Roddick was now in the finals and his opponent was the ever-dangerous Thai Paradorn Srichaphan. Ranked 11th in the world, Srichaphan had an excellent overall game including a formidable baseline game. The first set was a back and forth affair. Roddick and Scrichaphan held their own serves. With a swirling wind gusting, both men had service problems but somehow both managed to dominate their opponent with their service games. Scrichaphan had his best shot in the ninth game. In the previous game Roddick allowed Scrichaphan to escape. A disputed call got Roddick's ire, and he jawed with the judge. In the next game, Roddick calmed down and defended his serve. The first set ended in a tiebreaker. Roddick came out smoking in the tiebreaker. Holding his serve, he managed to take the first tiebreaker 7-2.

The second set began as the first ended, with Schrichaphan winning his first two-service games and Roddick winning his first two service games. Unless either man figured out how to break the other, another tiebreaker was inevitable.

In the fifth game, Roddick took advantage of Schrichaphan's mistakes as he broke the Thai. Roddick now had control being one break up. In the seventh game, Roddick came within one point of breaking Schrichaphan's service a second time, but Schrichaphan came back and held his service to stay within one game. Now he had to break Roddick but Roddick's service game was dominating as he took the eighth game; and in the tenth game, Roddick served out the match and won his third title in his last five tournaments.

Roddick told reporters, "I'm confident right now, and that makes a difference....I'm feeling good and thinking I'm going to win [every match]." Throughout the match, Roddick rushed the net and this strategy paid dividends. In the fifth game of the second set, this tactic unnerved the Thai and after Roddick broke the Thai's service game, it became Roddick's game to lose.

After the match, Roddick said, "Paradorn likes to chip his returns, so I thought I could get in there and not leave too much of the court open. That had a lot to do with the victory today." This was Roddick's third victory over the Thai. The 24-year-old Schrichaphan stated, "The windy conditions made it tough, but Andy was just too good." This was the first in a series of four hard court tournaments in preparation for the U.S. Open.

Part Three: Roddick in D.C.

It was the Legg Mason tournament; a tournament owned by SFX—the agency that represented Andy. You could say, the Legg Mason was a SFX all-star tournament with many of their players participating. Andy Roddick was the second seed behind Andre Agassi and, like Andre, had a bye till the second round when he faced Bob Bryan, a doubles specialist and part of the Bryan twin doubles team.

The court was fast and Bob Bryan matched Roddick, serve for serve, stroke for stroke. Neither man could gain the advantage over the other as the 205th ranked Bryan forced a tiebreaker, which proved as tight as the first set. Bryan served first and scored first blood as he moved ahead 1-0. Roddick took the next two service games and now it was 2-1. Bryan lost a serve and was down by one point but immediately took it back, tying the tiebreaker. Roddick served to take a one-point lead but Bryan's next serve tied the score. Roddick broke Bryan's serve and then took a 6-4 lead, needing one point to win. Bryan dug in and took the next point but Roddick finally prevailed 7-5 in the tiebreaker. In the second set, Roddick finally broke Bryan's serve and took the second set 6-4.

After the match, Roddick said of his opponent, "If he [Bob Bryan] takes a couple of months off of doubles and concentrates on singles, he could be a solid singles player. He played like a Top 35-40 singles player in the world tonight. I was very impressed the way he played out there. He just doesn't play singles enough." (Bryan along with his twin brother are one of the best doubles teams in the world.) Bryan was repeatedly hitting first serves in the 125-130 mph range, showing a power game that was competitive with Roddick's games. Now the next match was a rematch with Greg Rusedski, the British power server. Before the match, Roddick said, "There's not much game plan against Greg and he will try to dictate play on his serve and I hope to take care of my serve. I expect another tough match with him."

Andy began quickly as his service game was clicking and broke Rusedski's first service game to take a 3 games to 0 lead. Rusedski preserved his next service game though Andy would easily take his third service game of the set. Rusedski countered with a brilliant service game of his own to gain a little composure back. In the seventh game, Andy dominated his service game once more and from this point on both men held serve for the rest of the match. Unfortunately for Rusedski, having lost his first service game cost him the first set 6-3.

As for the second set, the game settled into the pattern of their previous match with neither man gaining an advantage over the other. Past duels were foremost on the fans minds as one fan yelled, "Well done, well done!" in reference to Rusedski's retort to the referee in his famous meltdown at Wimbledon. The second set was now a tiebreaker. Rusedski had to win to stay in the match and force a third set. For Andy, he wanted to end it now. In their previous match, Roddick made the big shots in the tiebreakers and wanted to repeat that here.

The key point came as Andy was up 4-3. Andy returned a Rusedski serve with a brilliant backhand passing shot just out of the Brit's reach. Roddick's booming serve ended the tiebreaker and Andy marched into the quarterfinals against his friend, Mardy Fish.

Friday afternoon in DC featured rain, and both Fish and Roddick found delays before and during the match. Roddick opened up quick, taking a 5-1 lead before a rain deluge halted the match. After an hour's break, both players came back with Roddick serving out the set. The next set began with Fish winning his first service game and serving notice that the next set would be more difficult than the first. Both men split their first two-service game before Roddick broke through in game five and once again, he had the advantage. Behind one game, Fish had to find a way to break through Roddick's service game, or else the match was over. Fish failed to find the answer to Roddick's serve and Roddick merely had to hold his own service game.

Andy Roddick began his semi finals match as if he had a date blowing British Tim Henman away in the first set 6-1. Henman had won only one match out of the previous five matches on hard court. It took only 24 minutes and Roddick only faced one break point.

The second set proved to be different as Henman regained his composure and Roddick started to lose his. Henman broke Roddick's serve in the fourth game when he nailed a forehand winner that Roddick thought was out. Roddick whacked the ball to the top of the stadium in disgust. Henman went on to close out the set 6-3.

The final set found each man defending his service game. Roddick regained his service game and lost just five points on his service game in the entire set. The key to the match came when Roddick failed to win his only break point of the set. Up 5 games to four, Roddick had his chance to win the match and march into the finals. Roddick returned Henman's forehand into the net. Henman forced the third set into a tiebreaker. Roddick took the first point with a vicious serve but then the Brit ran off seven straight points to win the match as Roddick continuously made groundstroke errors. Roddick's charge in D.C. and another match with Andre Agassi would have to wait until another day.

As for Henman, he was seeking his first title in the past year and a half. After the match, Henman told reporters, "I'm glad to say my shoulder is 100 percent. I've played well here and it couldn't have gone any better."

Henman added, "Andy was putting me under a lot of pressure. I made too many unforced errors…I was able to create some opportunities in the second set and once I had broken, I felt really happy with my own serve."

As for Roddick, this was only his second loss in the past 20 matches under Gilbert's tutelage. Now Roddick had two more warm ups before the United States Open.

Part Four: Roddick up North

The next step on the road to the US Open was the Montreal Masters with the first opponent being Xavier Malisse, who had yet to beat Roddick. Roddick opened the first set with an easy service game as he took a 1-0 lead, though the opening set proved difficult overall. In Roddick's second service game, he barely held and Malisse broke Roddick in the fifth game to take a 3-2 lead. Malisse was playing at his best and not only held his serve but broke Roddick twice as he won the first set 6-3. The Montreal Masters was a perfect test and the perfect preparation for the US Open as 19 of the top 20 players appeared and Malisse gave Andy a little test of what lay ahead. There would be no easy path to the finals.

After the match, Roddick commented about losing the first set, "I think I was just mad losing the first set. I don't think it's so bad when you're already down a break, but you just try to forget it as soon as possible."

Roddick began the second set breaking Malisse and then zipped through Malisse in his first service game. Roddick was now on a roll as he took Malisse's next service game. Malisse looked befuddled as Roddick took his game to a new level. This set ended 6-0 as Roddick pulled what some Tennis fans call a bagel (a shut out.)

Roddick was now hot and the momentum was in his favor. Malisse attempted to stem the tide with an opening victory in the first set as he had regained some steam back in his service game. Roddick shut out Malisse in his service game and then immediately broke Malisse to take command of the final set. Roddick then swept the next three games before Malisse stopped bleeding in the seventh game as Roddick served his way to victory. Roddick closed out the set with a tight final game as he was forced to deuce before finally prevailing. The final score for the set was 6-2. Next match was against Juan Chela of Argentina.

Juan Chela was an experienced clay player with his specialties being defense and returns. Chela's strategy was to "keep the ball in play and wait until your opponent makes a mistake.". Roddick could only manage four aces in the entire match.

The first match opened with Roddick winning the first game. Chela came back to tie and the match was on. Both men held their service game until Roddick broke through in the eighth game as Chela only scored one point. Roddick appeared to be in control until Chela came back to steal the serve back as he consistently out rallied the young American. The game headed to a tiebreaker.

Roddick hit the first serve dead on and took a 1-0 lead. Roddick took one of Chela's next two serves and nailed it. Roddick appeared in control 4-1. Chela then nailed his next serve and then broke Roddick's serve twice to take a 5-4 lead. The key moment came as Roddick broke Chela's serve and now the tiebreaker was dead even. Roddick hit Chela's next serve out and Chela was one point from the set. Roddick hit his serve and tied the match and then aced the Argentinean with Roddick now one point away. Chela hit his first serve in the net. Chela wound up and again, he hit the net. Double fault and Roddick prevailed.

Roddick broke Chela's first service game as he attempted to jump on Chela after the previous tense tiebreaker. In the fourth game, Roddick was one game ahead. They next had a great exchange in which Roddick hit three straight shots at the net and Chela returned them all with Chela trying to sneak one into the left corner. Roddick nailed the return right down the line with his left hand, a highlight shot.

Roddick then broke Chela a second time, and now was in command of the match. After an easy service game, Roddick went for the kill to end the match. Chela put on one last stand as he rallied to win the game and the set was 5-2 with Roddick serving for the match. Roddick nailed his service game and finished off the Argentinean 6-2 in the second set. After a tight first set, Roddick found his A game and dominated Chela; and now he was in the third round against Sebastian Grosjean.

Grosjean, like other Europeans, was trained on the clay and if nothing else, clay teaches patience. Grosjean first played Roddick in the Davis Cup, when he was victorious, but this was the only time he emerged triumphant over Roddick.

Roddick began the match with an overpowering serve as he closed out the first game with two aces. Grosjean won his first service game but in the fourth game, Roddick broke through and was a break up. Roddick took a 4-1 lead as he won an easy service game. Grosjean took four out of five points in the sixth game. Roddick dominated his next service, which included a smash that ended up in the second row after bouncing off Grosjean's racket.

Grosjean needed to hold serve to keep the set going and managed to stave off a defeat in the first set. Roddick needed to serve the set out, and at 30-15, he nailed a bullet to the corner and concluded the set with another smash that landed in the stadium.

Roddick now had the first set, 6-3 and it was time to close the show. Grosjean won the first three points of the first game but Roddick came back to make it deuce before Grosjean could serve out the game. Roddick's first service game of the set was as rough, as Roddick was forced to deuce before he smashed two powerful serves to end the game.

Grosjean's finesse game was starting to show as Grosjean showed patience and solid defensive skills including a big smash as he won the third game of the set. Roddick now served to tie the set and the power showed as he simply overwhelmed the Frenchman. The Frenchman managed to hold his next service game as his speed was threatening to become a factor in the match. Roddick held his service game to keep the set even. The next game was the crucial game that sealed Grosjean's fate as Roddick nailed the first three points against Grosjean's serve. Roddick broke Grosjean's serve with a brilliant shot down the line after reaching for Grosjean's shot over the net.

Now Grosjean had to do something that he had failed to do all match—break Roddick or it was over. Roddick had to merely hold his serve to close out the show and his service game was clicking. Grosjean made one last effort to win as he ripped three winners against the Roddick serve. Roddick dug in as he swept the next five points and the game concluded with a Grosjean shot into the net.

Grosjean attempted one more time to hold serve and took a 40-15 lead. Roddick dug in and forced deuce. Grosjean nailed a winner cross court to take the advantage but Roddick forced deuce with some great returns and Grosjean hit the ball out. Grosjean missed the next return out and the game ended not with a bang but a whimper as Grosjean double faulted to end the match. After the match, Roddick said, "You always know Sebastian is going to give 100 per cent. He is a very tricky player; he has a huge forehand when he gets set up. It could have gone either way tonight, because I was down love-40 a couple of times on my serve and then, you know, I hit a couple little dinky passing shots to break him a couple of times, so it probably was a lot tougher than the score indicates." Roddick now faced the Slovak veteran Karol Kurcera in the quarterfinals.

Kurcera began the match by breaking Roddick, jumping to a 1-0 lead, and then proceeding to take his first service game 2-0. In the fourth game, Roddick broke

Kurcera back and now the first set was tied 2-2. While Roddick defended his next service game, Kurcera showed defensive skills as he forced Roddick on his heels. Kurcera won this game with an ace and the match stayed on serve.

Roddick started his next service game on edge and Kurcera played the young American tough though Roddick prevailed with a winning shot cross-court. In the tenth game, Kurcera staved off three set points to prevent Roddick from breaking his serve. Roddick took the next service game with a clean ace and power-serve that Kurcera hit in the net. Kurerca forced a tiebreak.

Roddick lost his chance to control the tiebreak as he missed his first serve. Kurcera tied 3-3 with a cross-court shot. Roddick took a 5-4 lead on a searing ace. Kurcera won the next point as he forced Roddick into the net. Roddick won the next point off Kurcera's serve and when Kurcera returned Roddick's serve into the net Roddick prevailed 7-5.

Roddick opened the second set by stealing Kurcera's first game and ended the second game with an ace as he took a 2-0 lead. In the third game Kurcera opened the game with a slice over the net, catching Roddick off guard, and Kurcera had Roddick running all over the place as he won to stay in the match. Roddick easily won his service game but Kurcera rushed to a 40-0 lead before Roddick made it 40-30. Roddick shanked the last Kurcera serve out and now the match moved to the sixth game with Roddick holding the advantage. Roddick took the first two points and was looking to break Kurcera. Kurcera, however held on as he came back to score the next five out of six points.

Roddick ended the eighth game with an ace, and was now up 5 games to three. Kurcera had to win his serve and find a way to break Andy. Not since the first game of the match had Kurcera broken Andy's serve. Andy opened the final game with a shot down the line and then Kurcera returned an Andy forehand into the net. Kurcera then double faulted twice and Roddick was in the semifinals for a rematch with Roger Federer, his conqueror at Wimbledon.

There are matches in which a young player must be judged. In boxing, a prospect moves up the ladder and there is a point when potential must be turned into results. The first step before jumping into the upper echelons is the match against the wily veteran. Here many a prospect disappears but if the prospect prevails, the next step is the challenge to the upper echelon. A young Tennis prospect faces a similar task, for to join the upper echelon, you have to beat the best—no longer be satisfied with being just competitive. For Roddick, his first victory over Agassi in England at the Queens tournament was one such step. His semi-finals match with Federer another. Unlike Agassi, who at 33, is close to the end of his career, Federer was Roddick's age and both men would be facing each other in big matches for years to come. Roddick needed to show that he could beat the Swiss, for Federer would be a serious obstacle to Roddick winning a major since Federer had triumphed in their previous four meetings,

The semi was a tough match. Roddick in the first set took command as he broke Federer early. In the eighth game, he easily won his service game and took a 5-3 lead and took the first set.

The third set began with Federer breaking Roddick and then defending his service game. Federer was now in control of the final set and the momentum that he gained in winning the second set continued. Roddick managed to salvage his next service game but Federer once again defended serve and was ahead 3-1. Roddick needed a break but could not get one in the sixth game. In the eighth game, Roddick broke through as he finally broke Federer's service game for the first time since early in the first set. Now both men had broken each other once and the match was back on service. Federer defended his service game and Roddick his. Roddick attempted to gain the upper hand but failed as Federer rescued his game and Roddick was forced once more to defend his service game in order to send it to a tiebreaker. His service game clicked as Federer found it hard to return Roddick's bullet. Roddick forced a tiebreaker. Now seven points stood between Roddick and his first victory against Federer. Roddick not only has yet to beat Federer, but he has never won a tiebreaker against the Swiss.

Roddick nailed a sharp serve that zipped past Federer. Federer double faulted for the tenth time on his first serve in the tiebreaker. This was Federer's tenth double fault of the match. Roddick returned Federer's next serve down the line with Roddick now in control of the tiebreaker 3-0. Roddick's next serve hit handcuffed Federer and it was 4-0. Federer hit Roddick's next serve down the line, and he was still in the match. Roddick hit Federer's next serve into the net and it was 4-2. Roddick managed to score on Federer's next service game and it was 5-2 with Roddick needing two serves to prevail.

Federer stayed in the match as he zipped a forehand past Roddick's outstretched racket. Roddick's next serve once again hit Federer's backhand. The score was 6-3 and Roddick was one match point away but Federer had two serves to tighten the match. With his girlfriend looking over his shoulder, Roddick waited for Federer's next serve. Federer nailed it to Roddick backhand, which then zipped past the net into Federer's forehand. Federer attempted to guide the ball right into the corner but it sailed right past the out line and Roddick had his first victory over Federer. After the match, Federer said, "I made a few double faults, but it happened because I wanted to take some risks, I wanted to take control because I didn't wish to get into rallies against him." Roddick added, "It definitely wasn't looking good out there, but to win a match where I was down and fought back and clawed and scrapped feels good."

Now it was on to the finals to face David Nalbandian, who upset the German Rainer Schuettler. For Roddick a victory in the finals would represent Andy's fourth tournament win in his last seven tournaments.

The finals match was not just between Nalbandian and Roddick but, players against nature, as rain delayed the match. When the match began, Andy held his first serve and then broke the Argentinean to take a 2-0 lead. Next game, Andy just ripped into Nalbandian as he had a love game. Nalbandian managed to win his first service game but that was it as Roddick dominated the rest of the set to take it 6-1.

Roddick began the second set with a service break, but Nalbandian returned the favor and evened the set 1-1. Roddick managed to break Nalbandian as neither player could seem to defend his service game. Roddick held his next service game and he was in control of the set. All he had to do was to hold his service game. After the six games, Roddick held a 4-2 lead in games before once again the rain came streaming down, with both men heading for cover. After the rain, Nalbandian served to stay in the game. Roddick easily won the eighth game, and Nalbandian not only needed to hold his serve but also had to break Roddick's one more time in this set. Nalbandian hit a Roddick service return into the net, and his next shot went wide; and before Nalbandian knew it, he was one point away from losing the match. Nalbandian managed to score the next point, but his last shot went into the net and Roddick had his fourth title of the year. It was his first Masters, and this Masters victory had the air of a majors with almost every major star there. Roddick passed his dress rehearsal for the US Open with flying colors. Next stop was Cincinnati. Roddick had his first Masters victory.

Part Five: Cincinnati Masters

Before Roddick began his run at the Cincinnati Western and Southern Financial Group Masters, surprises had already occurred. Moya and Hewitt had already left and Federer came within a point of being eliminated earlier that morning. Seeded players were being left in the dust, one after another.

Roddick's first opponent was the left-handed Spanish player Fernando Verdasco, who had to beat Alexander Pope just to get into the round of 64. Roddick opened up fast as he closed out the first game with two aces. After dropping the first point, the Spaniard came back and took his first service game. While Roddick easily defended his next service game, Verdasco fought off Roddick's charges as he hit a brilliant cross shot after placing Roddick out of position with swift maneuvering.

After an easy love game for Roddick, Verdasco came back to tie up the set. Roddick started his next game with two aces, the last being 130 mph. After Verdasco tied it, Roddick finished it out with two more booming serves as Verdasco weakly tapped Roddick's last serve into the net.

Roddick broke Verdasco's service game with a brilliant play as he twice ran down Verdasco's drop shots before nailing a shot down the line. Now it was time to serve it out. Roddick did just that, served it in a love game as Verdasco barely reached Roddick's serve with it just sputtering into the net.

With one set in the bag, Roddick needed one more to advance. The opening game was nip and tuck as Verdasco fell behind 30-40. The Spaniard came back and ended the game with a searing ace. Verdasco broke Roddick's serve and now was in command of the second set. Roddick dug in immediately, returning the favor as he nailed his first game of the set by sending a howling forehand down the line past Verdasco. Roddick tied the set as he nailed a 133 mph serve past Verdasco, who barely had time to lift his racket as the ball sailed past him.

Roddick broke Verdasco a second time as Verdasco sent a shot sailing past the end line. Now Roddick had control of the set and all he had to do was to hold serve and it was over. Roddick hit a perfect second serve that handcuffed Verdasco as Verdasco sent the last shot of the sixth game into the third row of the stands. It was now 4-2, Roddick. Roddick broke Verdasco a third time as he took a 5-2 lead going into his service game. Roddick swept through the first three points before Verdasco forced a Roddick shot into the net. Verdasco's next shot was over the line, and Roddick swept the last six games to win the set 6-2. Roddick survived the first test.

After the match, Roddick said, "Verdasco is a good young player. He hits the ball a ton. You definitely feel the weight of his shot when you're playing against him. You know, he's gonna win a lot of matches."

Roddick's next match was an easy 6-1, 6-4 victory over Ljubicic, dropping just five games the entire match and gaining control early in both sets. The Croatian never once broke Roddick's service game. As for the rest of the field, Roger Federer was eliminated along with Juan Carlos Ferrero. The first two rounds saw many of the heavy favorites eliminated; and now Roddick's along with Argentinean Guillermo Coria were the only major seeds left as they both entered the final round of 16.

Roddick's next match was with James Blake, who also swept through his previous match with the Dutch player, Sjeng Schalken. The match was scheduled to be the featured match of the day. Blake told reporters, "Andy's probably playing the best out of all the guys right now, but he's still beatable, still human. You know, his serve can go off—I hope—because it's almost impossible to return when he's serving well. But I've got to take my chances on that. When I get second chances, try to go after him, make him play, and then really concentrate hard."

About playing his Davis cup teammate and friend, James Blake, Roddick said, "We've had some very close matches before, a couple three-setters. You know, I think he's improving all the time as well, so every match is a new match. And I think, you know, the six times that I've beaten him are kind of maybe thrown out the window. I mean, it's a new match."

Roddick, with the field being depleted, was in a great position to win his second straight Masters event. However, Roddick was not thinking title as he warned reporters, "You know, to see the depth in men's tennis. It's been there for the last couple of years, you know, at various tournaments, you know. It's just that I don't think it's surprising so much as coincidental that, you know, in a tournament where maybe a couple seeds lose, maybe they all did. So, you know, I don't think "surprising" is the word." Roddick knew that in spite of the upsets, the path to the finals would still be difficult.

James Blake has lost six straight matches to Roddick and now it was time to change his luck. Blake started out fast and while he played beautiful defense upon his service game and Roddick first two services games, Blake had numerous opportunities to break Roddick. Blake had Roddick on his heels in the first set. Blake had more winners and even more aces as each man split their service games.

Roddick started the tiebreaker as Blake hit his first ball into the net and then sent a return sailing wide to fall behind 2-0. Roddick failed to return Blake's serve and it hit into the net. While Roddick's serve forced Blake to hit another ball wide, Blake broke Roddick's next serve and the tiebreaker was 3-2 with Blake holding the serve for the next two points. Blake however failed to take advantage as he hit his shot wide and then double faulted. Now it was Andy's match to win as he held the next two serves and a 5-2 lead. Andy ended the tiebreaker.

Roddick moved in for the kill in the second set as he went after Blake in Blake's service game. Blake's last shot of the first game went slightly over the line in a close call. (Replays showed later that Blake had a legitimate complaint, as his last shot was good.)

Roddick dominated his service game but Blake held his service game to stay in the match. After Roddick held his service game in the sixth game he held a 4-2 lead. Roddick was in control of the set and now Blake had to hold his serve and then break Roddick. Once again, Roddick took Blake's service game, his second of the set. Now Roddick was in a position to end the match. After two quick shots, Roddick held a 30-love lead. Blake made his last stand as he reversed the tide and took a 30-40 lead on Roddick's serve. Roddick forced deuce and then smashed two straight aces as he closed out the match. While the first set was close and Blake had opportunities to take it, Roddick took his game to another level in the second set.

After the match, Roddick said "Yeah, I thought James came out and definitely played a better first set than I did up till 6-all. He gave me a couple points in the tiebreaker—forehand went wide on him, and the double-fault. I don't think—I think his level dropped a little bit in the second and mine—I raised mine a little bit." He admitted, "He was getting the better of me in pretty much every situation. I didn't really have a sniff on his serve. He was in a lot of my service games. I was just hoping maybe get to a tiebreaker and hope what happened, you know, what ended up happening, would happen. You know, that's what I was telling myself."

Blake told reporters, "If he's having one of the two best serving days of his life, no one's beating him. Can't really fault myself for that. He's played well against me. Can't go home and cry about it; it happens."

The next match was with unseeded Mariano Zabaleta and Roddick started out fast, zipping to a 4 games to zip lead in the first set. Roddick's service game was clicking and Zabaleta was hard pressed to keep up. The only service game he took was in the fifth game, but the first set ended with Roddick 6-1. Roddick finished the first set in 23 minutes.

Zabaleta defended his first two service games and had a 2 to 1 lead. Roddick once again broke in the fifth game and from this point on, he controlled the set and the match as he won the second set 6-2.

The semi final match was between Roddick and Max "the beast" Mirnyi. The tall Mirnyi had a long wingspan that proved advantageous at the net. That long arm span virtually makes it difficult if not impossible to shoot anything past him. When Mirnyi was on, he virtually lived at the net. Roddick's's advantage was his big serve which could force Max back and keep him off the net.

The first set was a nip and tuck affair with each men playing to their strength. Roddick's power serve allowed him to defend his service games and Max Mirnyi attacked the net behind his serve and successfully cut the court size reducing the room in which Andy could shoot his powerful forehand return pass.

Both men exchanged games as the first set was decided by a tiebreaker. Mirnyi began the tiebreaker hot as he mixed his serve with an excellent net game racing to a 5-1 lead. The Belarus native now was two set points away. Roddick regained his groundstroke and then, behind his powerful serve, he scored the next 6 points, snatching victory from the jaws of defeat.

Andy then took command of the next set as he broke Max Mirnyi off the bat and with a powerful serve leading the way, he jumped to a 2 games to 0 lead in the second set.

Mirnyi took an easy love game as he got back in the set but was not able to break Roddick's's serve in the 4th game. Roddick, down 40-15, came back in the fight game to tie the game at deuce. Roddick was looking to clinch the victory with another break. Mirnyi regained his poise and defended his service game. In the sixth game, Mirnyi immediately smashed two strong forehands as he took the first two points of the game. Mirnyi after another excellent net game, now had one point to tie the set. Roddick shot a sizzling ace and from this point on, he managed to finish out the sixth game.

Mirnyi held his serve and Roddick repeated the feat in the eighth game as the score going into the ninth game was 5-3. Mirnyi kept the pressure on Roddick, his net play continuously pestering the younger American. Mirnyi now was just one game behind going in the tenth game of the set. Roddick needed to serve the game out and that is just what he did. Roddick came through 6-4 to take a two set victory. The score however did not tell the story of how closely Roddick was to losing the first set, and with only one break of service game, Roddick had to depend upon his own service game to keep Mirnyi off-balance.

After the match Roddick commented, "I mean when two guys are serving—I don't know if we both finished above 70, but we were pretty close. When two guys are serving like that, one break can make the match, and it did." Roddick was referring to his break of Mirnyi's serve in the first game of the second set, the only service break of the game. About being down 5-1 in the tiebreaker, Roddick said, "I definitely am not going to give myself great odds being down 5-1 in a breaker against Max. But I hung around and I made him play a little bit, and you know, I served well from there on out in the breaker."

When asked about the first tiebreaker, Max Mirnyi said, "Well, certainly being up 5-1 you like your chances winning a tiebreaker, no matter who you play, but I made an error with a fairly difficult volley at that point, and then he came up with a great passing shot, inside out forehand, if you remember, and then that let the court running backhand that he hit, so it was a string of a couple points that, you know, should have gone my way, but didn't." When asked about Roddick's's powerful serve, Mirnyi commented, "Well, actually, it is a powerful serve, but I've played with guys that have better serves. You know, it's—you know, he does win a lot of points with it, but there are guys that disguise it much better than he does, and I was not really impressed that much."

Roddick now was appearing in his second straight Masters final against Mardy Fish, an upset winner of seeded German player, Rainer Schuettler. Fish managed to take two close tiebreakers from Schuettler to set up an all-American finals with his fellow Floridian Andy Roddick.

Roddick discussed Mardy's match when he told reporters before the match, "He's a better player. He's learning, he's getting—most of all—I think he always had the ability. He can pick up a football and throw it spot on, and he's one of those guys who can take a pool shot and do it. He's talented in everything he does. I think it's just a matter of confidence." Roddick was the heavy favorite but knew that this would be a tough match. For Roddick, a victory would put him number one in the championship race so there was something at stake that extended beyond winning his second Masters in a row. He would also be the first player to win both the Canadian and Cincinnati Masters since Patrick Rafter in 1998 if he succeeded in defeating Mardy Fish. Roddick had to beat a friend who he has known since childhood.

Mardy Fish was on a hot streak and had yet to lose a service game since his opening match. And, he began the opening set by challenging Andy's famous service game before succumbing. Then Andy returned the favor, taking Fish to deuce in the second game before Fish served out the game.

Fish broke Roddick's service game to take a 3 games to 2 lead as he jumped on Andy's serves with powerful forehands. Fish started to take command as Andy remained on the defensive throughout the first set. While Andy salvaged the rest of his service game, he could not break Fish's serve. While Fish did not have the power game of Andy Roddick, he still could put some mustard on it in the 125 mph range. Throughout the game, he played like the second coming of Pete Sampras as he matched Roddick serve for serve on occasion doing a Sampras leaping forehand smash. Roddick was playing back of the baseline and Fish took advantage of this by hitting the angles before Roddick and scoring with his two-handed backhand and forehand.

Fish won the first set 6-4 as he protected his serve. Fish began the second set as he did the first by dominating his service game. During the third game, Roddick had his chance to break Fish but Fish repeatedly came back to salvage the game. For the rest of the set, both men defended their service game but after the sixth game, Roddick had to fix his shoe and this break gave Roddick a chance to compose himself, while the frustration began to show on Roddick's face. After the break, Roddick smashed home two straight aces and appeared to have come back in force. Roddick had two break points but again Fish fought back. Roddick did a quick love game to take a 5 game to 4 lead but Fish returned the favor. The second set ended up in a tiebreaker.

Roddick began the tiebreaker by taking the opening serve and took a 2-1 lead as Fish hit a Roddick return back into the net. Fish managed to take Roddick's serve as he smashed a return down the line, but his next return went wide and Roddick maintained a shaky 3-2 lead. Fish tied the game with an excellent serve that Roddick failed to return, but Roddick broke Fish's serve as Fish hit a Roddick serve wide right.

Roddick now had the serve and the game in his hand and did not disappoint the crowd as he took the next two points. Behind 6-3, Fish needed to make his next two serves to stay in the game. Roddick was one point away from the set. Roddick returned Fish's serve and Fish returned the ball over the baseline and out. Roddick escaped with the second set.

Fish, however, was not bowed as he went back to take a one game lead in the final set by his own powerful service game. Roddick appeared once again back on his heel as he repeatedly had to fight off Fish's challenges in his service game. Both men held their service game but rallies became more frequent. In the fourth game, Fish returned Roddick's serves for points but not enough to take the game. Roddick and Fish both had opportunities to break each other throughout the set, but both men found the right serves to break the other's momentum. In the eighth game, a Roddick serve nailed Fish in the side and Fish buckled as if he was hit with a left hook. In the tenth game, Fish had two break points but Roddick managed to survive and the set was tied. In the twelfth game, Fish had a crucial match point twice but Roddick once again dug in to save the game.

Now it was a second tiebreaker and Roddick fell behind as Fish took the first point when Roddick's return went into the net. Roddick took a 2-1 lead as Fish's last shot went past the left line out. Roddick and Fish had a crucial exchange as both men zipped forehands at each other and rushed to the net. One, two, three strokes hit both men's rackets before Fish's last shot hit into the net. After the point, both men looked at each other and high fived one another. Roddick had a mini break and now he had a 3-2 lead. Fish had problem returning Roddick's next serve and then Roddick nailed a 129 mph ace for a 5-2 lead.

Fish stayed in the match as he outplayed Roddick on his next two-service game. With the score 5-4, Roddick had to serve the match out. Roddick got his sixth point as he nailed a perfect serve that Fish failed to return within the confines of the court. Now he was one point from his second Masters in a row. Roddick smashed a serve down the center and Fish returned the ball out over the baseline and it was over.

Roddick won this game without once breaking Fish but in the tiebreakers, he managed to make the big shots when it counted. Throughout the match, Fish outplayed Roddick but it was Roddick's play in the tiebreaker that determined the match.

About the play of his friend, Mardy Fish, Roddick said, "Mardy has improved so much even in a short space of time. I was proud of him." After an impressive summer, in which Roddick won three tournaments and one semifinal appearance, Roddick admitted, "Injury-wise, I'm fine—just fatigued. "I've played a lot of tennis in the last month, so it's going to be a good couple of days off now. I probably won't even touch a racket for the next two days."

Roddick now held the number one slot in the ATP champion race. He won his fifth title in the last eight tournaments. When Pat Rafter won both the Canadian and the Cincinnati Masters, he took the US Open as well. Would history repeat itself in 2003? As Roddick told reporters, "Everything that has happened this summer is out the door when you start a grand slam."

As for Gilbert, He noticed photographer Kat Donelson's visor that had the following phrase, "Bring back the Visor!" While signing Ms. Donelson's visor, he quipped, "Weak! Visors are weak! they're not for men. Visors are for ladies doubles." (For many Roddick fans, they love the visor, but Gilbert decided that the visor was not intimidating enough, and he was the deciding voice.)

Part Six: U.S. Open

It was the morning of August 20th and Roddick was the hottest option on Wall Street as he opened the Nasdaq. Coming from his second straight Masters win, Roddick was one of the heavy favorites for the US Open, though Tim Henman, the only man who beat Andy Roddick over the past month and a half, would be Roddick's scheduled first round opponent. Roddick's parents took Andy to his first open when he was nine, where he witnessed Jimmy Connors last charge at the age of 38. Now, he was one of the heavy favorites and while he was ranked number one in the championship race, Roger Federer, Juan Carlos Ferrero and Andre Agassi were close in the standings. If one of these top four won the US Open, they would have the number one ranking.

As Roddick prepared for the US Open, there was a difference in attitude from past US Opens. In a pre match interview, Roddick said, "You know, I probably didn't go into the last two Opens to win the tournament. I probably went in to make a good run. I definitely want to try to take this title. I know that's big talk, but I feel like I've played pretty well this summer. But first and foremost, I have to deal with Henman first round. He's a very good player, and I did lose to him in Washington, so that's where my focus is right now." When asked if he would be disappointed if he did not win, he replied, "If I play great tennis and beat really good players, obviously, you never know, but I'd definitely be disappointed. I definitely want to try to step up to the occasion and play well." Roddick discussed taking on the difficulty of following Sampras and Agassi, stating, "I was pretty lucky, Pete and Andre were both playing when I kind of started to make my move, and Andre is still playing great tennis. So, it's been kind of easier for me. Now I'm at the point where I feel like I am ready."

Roddick talked about Sampras's place in history as he told reporters, "He was just one of the most graceful players of all time, one of the most quietly competitive people of all time. And he's got to be one—when I think of him, I think of him as one best pressure players of all time. It seemed like the bigger the match was, the better that he played. You know, he just did it all in his own time. He didn't really make a big fuss about things. He just made his name by winning."

Opening day signaled the end of an era as Pete Sampras officially retired. For the past 12 years, Sampras was American Tennis. With a powerful serve and powerful forehand, Sampras would overwhelm his opponent and on the biggest stage of Tennis at the US Open and Wimbledon, he was the master. In the big matches, he played his best games. As Pete said his good byes, Roddick prepared for Tim Henman and now in some ways it was a role reversal. Tim Henman was used to being the man with a nation's hope on his back at Wimbledon. At this Open, it was Roddick who was slated to be the next Pete Sampras, America's big hope for this tournament.

Earlier in the afternoon, Michael Chang played his last Tennis at the Open. A comtempory of Pete Sampras and Andre Agassi, Chang was the first of that group to win a major. At the age of 17, He won the French Open and would never win another major. In 1996, he would have his best year with two major finals but no championship. While Agassi still was at the top of his game and even Todd Martin was still capable of advancing in a major, Chang was basically a one match and out. He did not have his old quickness and never had the power to play with the others. He depended on speed and endurance. What Chang had left in the end was endurance and heart and that was no longer enough. As Sampras and Chang exited stage left, Agassi and Martin were all that was left of the old lions from the past decade.

Tim Henman was the crafty veteran and somehow due to some peculiarity of the draw, Roddick found himself playing a man who normally would be seeded in the top ten. But due to injuries, Henman missed several tournaments early in the season. That caused Henman's ratings to drop when compared to previous years, though over the summer he was playing well.

Henman showed his craft early in the match as he forced Roddick to deuce in Roddick's first service game, but by the third game, Roddick got his first break as Henman doubled faulted the game away.

Henman on Roddick's next service game came back from two game points down to bring it back to deuce. Roddick prevailed but not before some anxious moments. In the sixth game, Roddick took the game with a brilliant backhand that went zipping past the charging Henman and Henman ended the game with a return into the net. During the seventh game, Tim Henman continued to charge the net, and on two different occasions cut off Roddick's angle for a return. While Roddick came back from two game points down to bring it deuce, Henman's craftiness came through as he concluded the seventh game with an eye dropper (which is another term for a drop shot just over the net.)

In the eighth game, Henman took a quick 0-30 lead before Roddick scored the next three point, but a double fault produced duece and on the next shot, Henman approached the net and nailed a perfect cross shot. Roddick eventually prevailed to take a 5 games to 3 lead but not before a few more anxious moments.

Roddick began to make Henman work on his serve and in the style of Andre Agassi, kept pressuring his opponent with his powerful forehand. Henman ended the set with a forehand that got away and Roddick snatched a first set victory by a score of 6-3.

Henman opened the second set by breaking Roddick. Roddick missed an easy shot and Henman gained an advantage. Henman's superior net game proved decisive as Roddick ended the first game with a forehand into the net.

Roddick had his chance to get the break back but Henman managed to come back from three break points to salvage his serve. Roddick marched through his next service game though to send a message, "I'm back" but somehow Henman's play was beginning to cause Roddick some concern. Henman's next game was a masterful show of movement as Roddick appeared to be one step behind his British opponent.

In the sixth game, Roddick began to show emotion as he nailed a backhand that Henman returned into the net and Roddick had his break to tie the set and then had a quick service game to take a 4 games to 3 advantage. He was looking to put the second set away.

Roddick continued putting the pressure on Henman as he once again had break points in a game and once again Henman managed to stave off a break. Henman then broke Roddick's service game a second time to take a 5 game to 4 lead.

The second set took on a look of desperation as both men struggled to gain advantage. Roddick beat Henman's next service game to stave off losing the second set and it was tied again. Neither man looked comfortable defending serve even though Roddick managed to scrape out the eleventh game. Now it was six games to five and this match began to take on the flavor of a later round match. Rarely does a first round features two superb players opposite one another. Henman brought the second set to a tiebreaker as he took his service game easily.

Roddick won the first point as Henman's return went long. Henman returned a Roddick forehand in the net and now Roddick was up 2-0. Henman survived a flurry of Roddick shots at net and hit a soft shot past the young American. Roddick took a 4-1 lead on a 140 mph serve that Henman barely got a racket on. Roddick nailed a powerful forehand on a Henman serve and took control of the tiebreaker. Roddick ended the tiebreaker with a powerful serve and now had the second set in hand. The tiebreaker was the key moment of the game. With Roddick appearing uncomfortable by Henman's aggressive style, Henman had the chance to tie the match and put pressure on Roddick. In his previous victory over Roddick, Henman lost the first set easily before coming back to take the next two sets, the last being a tiebreaker. Roddick's's gritty play and ability to make clutch shots allowed the young American to prevail. The tiebreak ended Henman's chance of upsetting Roddick and now the momentum was with Roddick.

Henman took the first game of the third set and Roddick ended the second game with two aces. Roddick apparently gained control of the third set after breaking Henman for a fourth time in the match in the third game as he took a 2 games to 1 lead. Now Roddick needed to control his serve and he was on his way to the second round. Roddick nailed a love game to take his third game of the set. Three more down. After Henman held on to his serve, Roddick nailed down another straight point game on his next serve.

As Roddick won the eighth game, his serve started to dominate with him losing only two points on his first previous five service games. Roddick now needed to win one more game to take the match and Tim Henman was serving to survive. Roddick dominated Henman's serve as he took three of the first four points. Henman was down two match points and needed two big serves just to bring the final game to deuce. Henman shot a serve down the middle and Roddick nailed a backhand back to Henman's backhand. Henman's return went wide and the match was over. 6-3, 7-6, 6-3, Roddick triumphed over a tough foe and overcome a rough hurdle.

Talking about strategy with the press after the match, Roddick said, "In Washington I made the mistake of giving him one pace, one pace, one pace, one pace. He's not easy to overpower because he feels the ball so well. That was definitely something I had to do tonight."

Roddick's's next opponent was Croatian Ivan Ljubicic and Roddick took the first game. Roddick took the first three points but Ljubicic came back to bring it to deuce and using his own powerful serve tied the set up.

Roddick ended his second service game with an easy drop shot that caught Ljubicic unaware. Then Roddick broke Ljubicic with a crosscourt beauty and took a 3 games to 1 lead. Roddick appeared to be in control of the set until the ninth game as Ljubicic was three break points away from taking a service game. Roddick came back though with several overpowering serves reaching mid 130's. Roddick garnered five straight points to end the set.

The second set began with an easy service game by Ljubicic, and Roddick struggled to maintain his service game. In the third game, Roddick started out with triple break point that included a spectacular shot down the line. Ljubicic brought the game back to deuce and both men literally pounded each other before Roddick broke Ljubicic's serve in the second set.

Roddick took his next service game and once again appeared to be in control of the set. Ljubicic broke Roddick back and now the score was tied 3 games apiece. Ljubicic began to look more confident and Roddick appeared flat on his heels as the Croatian was putting his own service game together.

In the tenth game, Ljubicic had three set break points but Roddick roared back to save the set for the moment. Both men exchanged service games and now it went to tiebreak.

Roddick returned Ljubicic's first serve into the net. As Roddick took the next point, Roddick hit a return that nicked the net and stayed on his side. Ljubicic hit a perfect drop and then a solid serve that was returned out by Roddick. Ljubicic nailed a Roddick serve perfectly and only Roddick's serve saved the tiebreak for the moment.

Ljubicic now was one set point away after a brilliant backhand return. Roddick now had three set points to save. Roddick saved the first point as Ljubicic's return went into the net. Ljubicic won the tiebreaker as Roddick's return went wide.

Roddick opened the third set with three aces and an easy service game. On the fourth game, Roddick once again broke Ljubicic and once again had control of the set. Roddick ended the fifth game with an ace and had a 4 games to 1 lead. Both players exchanged service game and now Roddick had his chance in the ninth game to end the set. Roddick ended the set with an ace. He had his momentum back as Ljubicic started to show signs of wear. During one break, Ljubicic had the trainer check his quads and he took an antacid for his stomach.

At the beginning of the fourth set, a trainer went out to check Roddick's arm. Both men were paying for their efforts. As the fourth set progressed, both men's service game took over and they proved to be overwhelming. In the seventh game, Roddick appeared to be breaking through Ljubicic's serve, but Ljubicic righted the ship after a Roddick lob shot that hit inside the back line tied the game 30-30. Roddick came back to tie the match with love game that ended with an ace.

From this point on, the service game continued to be dominant for both men. Roddick throughout the game stood some ten feet behind the baseline due to Ljubicic's power serve, which at times could match Roddick's. Ljubicic on occasion would take advantage of this by coming behind his serve and attacking the net. There were times when Roddick proved vulnerable to the drop shot as he had to cover considerable ground from the baseline. Both men had 22 aces against one another.

Once again there was a tiebreak, and Ljubicic started it with an ace. Roddick smashed an overhead shot to tie the score 1-1. Roddick took a 2-1 lead on a wicked serve that Ljubicic barely could touch. Ljubicic nailed another ace to tie the score 2-2. Ljubicic nailed an overhand shot after a brief rally to push ahead 3-2. Then Ljubicic nailed a backhand on a Roddick return and moved ahead 4-2 on a mini break as Roddick's shot sailed over the baseline. Roddick appeared to be tiring as his next return went into the net. Roddick lost both serves and now Ljubicic had the advantage and the serve. Ljubicic double faulted to keep Roddick in the tiebreak at 5-3. With the double-fault, Ljubicic provided Roddick with a gift. Ljubicic placed a drop shot that Roddick returned into the net. Now down 6-3, Roddick had to stave off three set points just to keep this match from going to a fifth set. Ljubicic barely missed a cross shot as Roddick took one of the needed three points. An ace gave him his second needed point and now Roddick needed one more point to keep this set from ending. Roddick tied the game as Ljubicic hit a return into the net. Ljubicic managed to take a 7-6 lead as he maneuvered Roddick out of position. Roddick followed up with a hard serve and a hard return out of reach of Ljubuicic's outstretched racket to tie the score, with Ljubicic complaining about the hard return that tied the score. (The replay showed Roddick's point was good.) Roddick nailed a 138 mph serve to take the lead at 8-7. Ljubicic rushed to the net after his serve and tied the game after a furious exchange. Roddick won the next point on Ljubicic's serve as he nailed the return with a crushing forehand into the corner. Roddick had match point, again. On the next point, Ljubicic rushed to the net and tried to loop over Roddick's head but it went out and Roddick nailed the victory.

Roddick prevailed but Ljubicic's powerful serves and forehands kept the pressure on Roddick. Roddick passed another test but Ljubicic was irritated with the more demonstrative Roddick after the match.

After the match, Ljubuicic said, "Well, I think that anywhere in the world, except in the United States, if we played this match I won it." He added, "I mean, generally, I don't like him. I mean, not me, nobody in the locker room likes his acting on the court. But that's not—I mean, he's a good player. He's gonna win a lot of matches, but not because he's like that. It's just that we don't like it. Because nobody acts like that. He's the only one."

Ljubuicic essentially stated that Roddick benefited from home court advantage as he declared, "It's—he's just—he doesn't respect the others, that's all what I can say. You know, it's not in your face or it's not in your face, doesn't matter. It's just that it's not—well, some other player's going in your face and you understand that they just want to win a match. But what he's doing is just pumping up the crowd, which is, in the United States he can do it. But everywhere else, if he does it, the people smiled, you know. Just like that. Fortunately for him, there is like 70 percent of the big tournaments are playing in the States. He's No. 4 in the world for that." Ljubuicic felt that Roddick's enthusiasm affected the judges decision on close decisions. Ljubuicic complained, "That was the crucial point, obviously. I am expecting some bad calls. But, you know, it hurts when it happens in the crucial moment like that."

While Ljubuicic was fuming in his press conference, Roddick merely rolled with the punches and for the most part ignored the criticism. Roddick said of his opponent, "It was a very tough match. Ivan's a very good player. I have tons of respect for him as a player. He has a huge serve. I thought he played very well from the baseline today. I've lost to him before. I was definitely skeptical coming in."

About the Ljubuicic complaints, Roddick merely responded, "I think that's pretty much sour grapes. You know, I don't know how—I don't know if I yelled "yes" before the linesman even called that ball or anything. I mean, I think the linesmen do their job. You know, I don't know if anybody saw the replay, but I'm pretty confident that that ball wasn't out. Maybe he was hoping it was out.

You know, that really doesn't deserve a response. I don't think that's very respectful. I definitely don't have anything bad to say about him. So it's disappointing."

As for his game, Roddick said, "It was a mixture. I was in control of things early, then, I played a bad game in the second set on my serve. From there on, he definitely lifted his level. I think if I would have held out the second set, I mean, then it's 3 and 3, you're looking pretty going into the third. But I played a bad game. I let him back into it. Then in the tiebreaker he played really good tennis and he started playing a lot better." As for his next opponent, Roddick commented, "It's tough. It's gonna be a lot different than the first two matches I've played. He'll stay at the baseline, you know. He's not gonna—I'm gonna get a look every return game. He's not gonna just put forcers by me where I don't really get my feet in the game. But, you know, he's flashy. He's pretty talented. You know, it's gonna be tough."

Shortly after 1:30 Roddick called Ljubicic about Ljuubicic's outburst with the idea to see what it was that bothered Ljubicic. Ljubicic asked Roddick, "Andy, why do you care what the others think about you?" Roddick replied, "I don't care." Ljubicic responded, "You really care. You're calling in the middle of the night to hear what somebody said about you in a press conference."

While some made this outburst into some sort of symbolism, the rich American vs. the poor Croatian who escaped death in the Balkans as a child, Ljubicic's outburst was no more than the outburst of a frustrated tennis player who gave all he got and lost a close battle.

This incident demonstrated a side of Roddick that very few know. When Roddick hired Brad Gilbert, he personally visited with his old coach Tarik Benhabiles to explain the decision. Maybe it is the old Midwest value that came into play but Roddick never took the easy way in dealing with personal issues. Fire a coach, you talk to the coach directly. Tarik was the man who took Roddick to the cusp of greatness and Tarik was not just Roddick's coach but protector. The decision to go with Gilbert was part of going to the next step in the upper echelon. So it was important for Roddick to talk with Tarik directly, and Roddick also felt it was important to deal with Ljubicic directly. Interesting, many of the details of the Ljubicic-Roddick discussion came from Ljubicic in a New York Times interview. While Roddick wanted to keep the matter private, the Croatian was willing to go public.

Ljubicic was less angry as Saturday dawned, though he told reporters the next day, "I had an opinion about him on the court, but it's not about him off of it. I have no problem with him in that way, but we are different." While Ljubicic was mollified by Roddick's gesture, it was clear that he still was not apologetic about his outburst. He told one reporter, "I really feel that I didn't say anything bad about him as a person. So he didn't ask for an apology, and I didn't feel like doing it. I'm telling you, we cleared the things. We talked last night, and I told him this morning, he came—I ask if everything okay. He said it's fine. Was probably some misunderstanding. I mean, I didn't say that he's ugly, I don't know, something I have to apologize."

Flavio Saretta was Roddick's next opponent and the first two games saw both men hold their service game easily. Saretta played from the baseline and his strategy was a defensive one with the idea of withstanding the Roddick onslaught. During the fourth game, Roddick produced the first service break as Saretta hit a Roddick forehand return into the net. Throughout the first set, Roddick had only given up one service point as he was varying his serve. In the sixth game, Roddick broke Saretta one more time, and appeared to be overpowering the Brazilian. Saretta's defensive strategy was falling apart and Roddick's power was putting the Brazilian on his heel. Saretta had no answer in the early going.

After taking the first set easily 6-1, Roddick broke Saretta off the bat to take a quick 1 game to 0 lead. Then Roddick's next service game was an easy love game with a couple of 135 mph serves thrown in. While Saretta held his service game, Roddick ended the fourth game with a 136 mph ace. In the seventh game, Roddick had yet another break point capturing another Saretta service game though Saretta managed to stave off the service break with two aces and an excellent serve to Roddick's backhand that went into the net. Saretta began to show life after being totally dominated for the first thirteen games. Ahead 5 games to 2, Roddick broke Saretta for the second time in the set, and was one set away from the final 16.

In the third set, Roddick gained control of the set as Saretta doublefaulted his second service game to fall behind 3 games to 1. The next game, Roddick had yet another love game that included one 140 mph ace. After the seventh game, Roddick was now in control of the match with a 5 game to 2 lead. He needed one more game to go for the match. He was looking for one more service break. Saretta, after following behind 15-40 on his serve, fought off two match points to stay in the contest. He prevailed after a couple of spirited rallies to save his service game. On Roddick next service game, Saretta made one last stand as he had two break points on Roddick. He was in a position to break Roddick for the first time in the match but he could not convert. Roddick ended the game with a sharp serve to Saretta's backhand that the Brazilian returned weakly into the net. Roddick was now in the top 16.

After the match, Roddick said, "I don't think Flavio played his best tennis today. But I played pretty solid throughout the match, so that was okay." Roddick only made less than 60% of his first serves, but it was enough to dominate Saretta, who seemed a step slower than he was in earlier matches. Roddick said, "Actually, I didn't serve that high of a percentage today. I don't know if it got above 50. It was down in the 40s for a lot of the day. I was hitting my spots when I was making it. That was good." Roddick waited for the winner of the Malisse-Tursunov match.

Labor Day saw a deluge from the sky with most of the matches canceled. Only one match was completed on the women's side. None of the men's matches were completed and Tuesday was no better. Andre Agassi struggled against Taylor Dent and the weather. Dent was down 5 games to 4 before he came back and won the last three out of four games. As mist came down, Taylor surprised Agassi in a tiebreaker. During the second set, Taylor's own hard play and the cool temperatures conspired against the young American as he pulled his hamstring. After losing both the second and third sets, he no longer could compete and Agassi squeezed by to reach the quarterfinals. Roddick was scheduled to play after the Agassi-Dent match but once again, the rain prevailed over the officials at the Open, as the Roddick-Malisse match was postponed along with the other men's matches.

Roddick in the meantime, played "correspondent" for Jim Rome's ESPN program, *Rome is Burning*. Roddick reviewed his time in New York beginning with his opening of the NASDQ market. Rome's people filmed Roddick practicing and trading quips with Gilbert.

After three days of rain, Roddick finally entered center stage against Xavier Malisse. Malisse had never defeated Roddick in their seven previous meetings, though Malisse felt that his time had come. For the first three games, neither man scored a point off the other before Roddick finally grabbed game four from Malisse. The early games found neither man warming up in the cool New York night, but finally Roddick started to take control in the first set even with the weather against him.

After winning the first set 6-3, Roddick had several break points against Malisse in the first game of the second set but could not quite break Malisse though he easily won his service game. By the third game, Malisse started to look comfortable as his service game began to look smooth. After Roddick defended his serve and had 0-15 advantage on Malisse's service game, the rain once again came down.

After yet another delay, the match began, again, as Malisse struggled to defend his serve down 0-15. After finally breaking Malisse in Malisse's next service game, another rain delay occurred. Behind 5 games to 3, Malisse defended his serve, forcing Roddick to serve for the set. Roddick served out the set and grabbed a two set lead and now had one set left to move into the quarterfinals. With the weather a question mark, Roddick wanted to end the match, for this would give him a day off. Another cancellation would mean that the winner would have to play four days in a row with no rest. Roddick only lost three points on his service game through the first two sets, demonstrating the power of his service game.

Malisse won the first game of the third set rather easily and ended the set with two aces. In Roddick's next service game, he made three difficult shots in the net look easy. Malisse on his next service had to fight off a Roddick break to stay on serve. With Roddick's service game at another level, Malisse was feeling the pressure of having to hold his serve to stay in the game. While Roddick was holding his serve with ease, Malisse was forced to fend off break points on his. In the third set, Malisse dug in with the idea of getting the third set into a tiebreaker where anything can happen. In the eighth game, Malisse rallied and managed to get three break points on Roddick's service game before Roddick prevailed.

On Roddick's next service game, Malisse had two more break points before Roddick fought him back. After Malisse won the eleventh game to take a 6 games to 5 lead, Roddick had to win his service game to push it to a tiebreak, doing just that after defending his service game. Malisse had an easy point lined up but pushed the ball into the net and Roddick had the first point. Roddick hit a return out of bounds before taking the next point. Malisse now had the serve down 2-1. Malisse maneuvered Roddick out of position as he hit a floater into the middle and followed that up with an ace to take a 3-2 lead. Malisse and Roddick rallied as each other nailed shots, before Roddick rushed the net with a drop shot for the point. Roddick made another mistake as his shot whistled out and Malisse had the advantage. Malisse nailed a wicked serve that an off balance Roddick hit out. Roddick gathered the next point to get the tiebreak back on serve. Roddick nailed a big serve to tie the tiebreak 5-5. Malisse hit a long shot and now Roddick had a match point. Malisse had the ball in his hand for the serve. Malisse and Roddick had one tough rally as both men pounded the baseline. Roddick hit a solid passing shot that Malisse hit into the net as he was rushing the net.

Roddick had reached the quarters three years in a row, but unlike past years, this felt different. Over the past two Opens, he would lose to the eventual champion but this year it was he who was the favorite. After the match, Roddick said, "Yeah, I want to get through this year. I feel like I'm playing a lot better than I had in any of the other years. I'm healthy this year. Last year I was a little banged up going into the quarters. So I feel good." When he fell behind in the tiebreak 5-3, Roddick admitted, "Yeah, I was down 5-3 and serving. I wasn't exactly liking my prospects at that point. You can't really think about, "Oh, that might slip away." You just got to say, "Okay, I'm down 5-3, down one mini break."

About the key moment when he held a 5-3 lead and serving, Malisse said, "Well, I lost the point. And, you know, we played a rally. I should have probably just made the backhand. You know, after that, you see I try to make the passing shot. I missed it. I can't really say anything about it because he attacked. I tried to counterattack. I missed it. I tried to make it. It's just well-played of him, putting pressure on at the right time. You know, he just played a good point."

About Roddick's game, Malisse told reporters, "He served too good in the first two sets. I think the third set I started returning a lot better, blocking the serves. On the five breakpoints, you know, he played well on all five and maybe one on the second serves, on the set point. I just clipped the tape. But otherwise he played well. So it's not like I made the mistake or anything. I think today he deserved to win."

Roddick now faced the Dutch player, Sjeng Schalken, and Roddick had beaten Schalken two out of their three previous meetings, though Schalken made it to the US Open semifinals last year, which was farther that Roddick had gone. The first five games of the first set stayed on serve before Roddick broke through Schalken's service game to take a two game advantage. With Roddick in control of the set and taking a quick 30-0 lead, Schalken produced his own shock and awe as he broke Roddick's serve, the first service game that Roddick lost in his last 47 games. Roddick returned the favor and closed out the first set with his second break.

Roddick once again gained the upper hand in the second set as he broke Schalken in the fourth game of that set, as a Schalken second serve was returned with mustard by Roddick. Schalken returned the Roddick forehand into the net and fell behind 3 games to 1. Roddick continued to steam roll through the set as he took the second set 6 games to 2. He ended the set by breaking Schalken a second time for the set. Roddick nailed a forehand down the line that Schalken returned out for the last point of the set. Now Roddick was one set away from his first US Open semifinals and his third major semifinal of the year.

In the fourth game of the third set, Roddick once again took a service game from Schalken and Schalken weakly returned a Roddick forehand into the net after a brief rally. Schalken could not even score a point on his serve, and then Roddick had another easy service game, including a 140 mph shot that handcuffed Schalken. Roddick was now two games from ending the match.

Schalken defended his next service game and opened up a 0-40 lead on Roddick's next service game. Roddick immediately got the game back to deuce with two straight aces and a Schalken return that went wide. Despite having four break points in the set, Schalken could not convert on any of his break points, and his last shot meekly went into the net. Schalken had a golden moment to put the third set back on serve with a chance of putting the set into a tiebreaker, but despite some shakiness by Roddick, Schalken could not dent Roddick's service game.

Schalken defended his service game despite one Roddick soaring forehand return that announcer John McEnroe wisecracked, "went 140 mph." Roddick served to finish out the set and match. Roddick sent a 139 mph serve right at Schalken, who barely got the ball over the net. Roddick sent the weak return sailing back and Schalken's racket barely touched the ball as it went softly into the net. Roddick now joined his fellow American Agassi in the semifinals. While Agassi would battle Juan Carlos Ferrero in one semi, Roddick waited for the winner of the David Nalbandian—Younes El Aynaoui match. Roddick was now one match from his first finals. After the match, Schalken stated, "He's playing too well for me at the moment—too well for a lot of guys."

Roddick faced David Nalbandian, who was coming off an upset win over Federer followed by a tough match against Younes El Aynaoui. As the match opened, both men held their serve, even though Roddick was forcing Nalbandian into long rallies. Roddick had his first major chance to break Nalbandian in the 5th game. He had 6 break points against Nalbandian but after a 22 point game, Nalbandian survived. This was the first turning point in the game as Nalbandian gained confidence that would continue for the first three sets.

After a Roddick hold in his service game, Nalbandian had his wrist wrapped due to soreness. In the eleventh game, Roddick started with three aces before Nalbandian put his racket on the ball. From this point on in the game, Nalbandian forced several long rallies and even had a break point before Roddick won. Nalbandian had to win his serve to force a tiebreaker. He did.

Nalbandian took the first two points of the tiebreak before Andy recovered his mini serve break. After Nalbandian nailed a backhand down the line, Roddick followed with an ace. Roddick tied the tiebreak when Nalbandian attempted a soft floater over Roddick's head but it went out. Roddick returned a Nalbandian forehand into the net. Nalbandian now had a 5-4 lead with the serve. Nalbandian, weak wrist and all, served out the tiebreak and took the first set.

Nalbandian once again saved a break point on his first service game to protect his service game as the second set began. Andy came back with a love game on his first service game in the second set. On Roddick's second service game, Andy played a more aggressive game as he rushed the net and changed his own pace.

In the sixth game, Nalbandian broke through Roddick's service game and now he was ahead 4 games to 2, and in control of the set and the match. Despite Roddick getting the next Nalbandian service to deuce, the Argentinean was able to nail a brilliant passing shot to end the game and take what appeared to be an overwhelming lead in the set. Roddick stayed in the set by acing Nalbandian for the 18th time in the match. Nalbandian played yet another brilliant service game as he took the second set 6-3 and appeared to be on his way to his second big upset of this US Open.

Roddick started the third set by winning his service game but Nalbandian appeared to have Roddick on his heels with Roddick appearing flatfooted in his next service game. Roddick served out his next game with three straight aces. At this point, Roddick took an injury time out to have foot blisters bandaged.

In the fifth game, Roddick was once again on the ropes as Nalbandian had two break points. Roddick saved his service game barely. In the seventh game, Nalbandian jumped out to a 30-15 lead and once again threatened to break yet another Roddick's service game. After two separate rallies, Nalbandian had yet another break point but Roddick once again preserved the serve. Nalbandian's strategy of just getting Roddick's power serve in play was working as he was now forcing Roddick in long rallies. As the set progressed, Roddick was still looking for his first service break against Nalbandian. After 10 games in the third set, Roddick was tied with Nalbandian.

Roddick had one more chance to break Nalbandian in the final game of the set, but Nalbandian stayed alive to force the second tiebreaker.

Roddick lost his first serve and fell quickly back 2-0 as he hit Nalbandian's serve out. Another Roddick return into the net after a long rally and Nalbandian was now ahead 3-0. Roddick scored on his next two serves and the score was 3-2. Nalbandian took a 4-2 lead with a passing shot in the corner after an 8 shot rally. Roddick stayed alive as Nalbandian hit a return into the net and the tiebreak was back on serve. Roddick took the next point to tie and now came a crucial serve. Roddick squeezed ahead 5-4 on his serve. Nalbandian took the next two points on his serves including a brilliant point that had Roddick shaking his head and wondering how Nalbandian's point stayed in. Nalbandian was now one point away from the match. Roddick was behind but he had the serve. An ace by Roddick tied it. A second ace put Roddick in the lead and gave him his first set point of the match.

Nalbandian tied it after a rally saw Roddick's return hit into the net. After Nalbandian hit a shot into the net, Roddick had the set point on his serve. A forehand shot by Roddick won the tiebreak and Roddick was still alive. This was the turning point of the match. When Nalbandian saved his serve in the first set after fighting off six break points, he took the momentum to dominate the next three sets. Roddick's ability to prevail in this tiebreak now gave the American the momentum to come back. But he still trailed two sets to one.

Roddick tried to ride the emotion of the tiebreak and managed to get two break points on Nalbandian's service game. Roddick finally broke Nalbandian for the first time in the match. The server held the next three games but as the fifth game approached, Roddick appeared to have momentum as he rushed to a quick 0-30 lead. And after two more points, Roddick had a double break point on Nalbandian's serve. After a Nalbandian double fault, Roddick had clear control of the set with a 4 games to 1 lead. Roddick put an exclamation mark on the match with an easy service game to move one game closer to the set. In the seventh game, Roddick had his third service break as he took an easy 6 games to 1 set to tie the match. After being unable to break Nalbandian in the first three games, he now broke Nalbandian three times in the set.

Roddick opened the fifth set by winning his service game. Nalbandian on his next service game found new life as he took a love game. Roddick held on to his serve with an ace but not before having to fight off Nalbandian rallies on the previous points. Nalbandian took two of the first three points and almost had another that missed the line by an inch. This was another crucial moment for if Nalbandian had a three-break point, he may have broken Roddick and taken control of the set and the match.

On Roddick's next serve, the game ended with Roddick barely reaching and pointing the ball just over the net as Nalbandian could not reach the ball. After the first six games, it was on serve as both men dug in their heels. Roddick, ever the showman, caught a ball in his hat that Nalbandian popped up after a shot was called out.

The seventh game ended when Nalbandian popped up his return out on a Roddick 126 mph serve, a game that featured Roddick 36th and 37th aces.

Roddick took a 15-30 lead with a high lofting shot that hit the back line. He then had two-breakpoints as he nailed a forehand in the corner. Roddick broke Nalbandian as the Argentinean's passing shot missed by an inch. Roddick had his service break and was serving for the finals. Roddick took a love service match but Nalbandian made some great returns and there were extended rallies but Roddick won as Nalbandian's last shot barely missed.

For Roddick, this match was a defining moment in the young American's career. Nalbandian played a brilliant game and had Roddick on the ropes in the first three sets. What kept Roddick in the game was his booming serve and powerful forehand. Throughout the match, Roddick had to call on his serve to bail him out. With 38 aces, Roddick counted on his serve to get out of trouble. Nalbandian's speed gave Roddick trouble throughout the match but in the end, Roddick dug in to pull out an improbable victory. Roddick attacked the net more than he had in the whole tournament and even scored 30 points in the net area—unRoddick like. Roddick showed that he could come back from a two set deficit at a crucial moment when being outplayed.

When asked about his slow start and falling behind to Nalbandian, Roddick said, "I think you have to give credit to David. I thought he played super well today. It's not like, you know, it was all me, the reason that I was down two sets. Especially, you know, I had that one game in the first set where I had a bunch of breakpoints and I didn't get it. After that I thought he started playing very, very well." When asked about how he felt falling behind and about his chances of coming back, Roddick responded, "I definitely wasn't feeling good about my prospects, but I didn't think it was 100 percent over. I just tried to play it point for point and not really worry about what had already transpired."

Nalbandian was disappointed after the loss and admitted that he was coping with a sore wrist and abdominal areas. About the match, Nalbandian stated, "Is difficult to play without serve and without backhand....It's also difficult play against Andy. He's a great player. So, many things." Nalbandian did complain about some of the calls as he commented, "Every time when it's close, everything is for them (Americans.)" Nalbandian nearly pulled off the upset and his performance showed the world that this Argentinean would soon be more than just a 13th seed in future majors.

Juan Carlos Ferrero came into the US Open finals as the top player in the world and Roddick came in number two. The US Open pitted against each other the men playing the best tennis in the world, and two men who never played against each other.

Roddick opened up with an easy service game but Juan Carlos countered with two aces in his first service as he held. This match featured Juan Carlos's speed vs. Roddick's power. Roddick drew first blood as he whipped a wicked forehand to conclude game four and broke Ferrero's service game. After a Roddick easy service game, Roddick threatened Ferrero's next service as he came back from 40-0 to bring it to deuce before Ferrero held on to hold service. Ferrero kept the set close and prevented a runaway in the first set.

Ferrero in his next service game whipped out two aces and had an easy love game and now needed to break Roddick to stay in the first set. Roddick had only lost one point in his previous service games, so the task in front of Ferrero was daunting. Roddick ended the set with two aces, one being 141 mph.

Ferrero started the second set with an easy hold. At this point, Ferrero was serving well except for one game, which cost him the first set. Roddick had an easy service game with three aces to tie the set. Ferrero was being blown away by the power of the Roddick serve, but was using his placement to make Roddick run on his serves and stay in the match.

Ferrero in the ninth game changed the pace as he nailed a perfect drop shot after following up on Roddick's backhand. He finished the game with a 125 mph ace, hard for the Spaniard. Roddick continued his dominance on his service game as he finished the tenth game with two aces. As Ferrero defended his service game, now Roddick had to hold to force a tiebreak.

After another Roddick hold of the serve, the tiebreak began with a Roddick whistling shot past Ferrero at the net. Ferrero nailed a cross-court forehand that slipped over the net and Roddick hit a return out as Ferrero took both of Roddick's serves to take a 2-1 lead. He had the advantage and the serve. Ferrero took his eye off the ball as he attempted a return of a Roddick forehand and sent the shot sailing high and out. On his next serve Ferrero went for a winner on a Roddick return and it went wide with Ferrero now down 3-2. Ferrero squandered his opportunities and Roddick made him pay. Roddick nailed an ace and now he was ahead 4-2. Roddick converted on another serve and now Ferrero was down 5-2. Ferrero on his next serve hit a Roddick return into the net and on Ferrero's next serve, Roddick nailed a shot down the corner to take the tiebreaker and a two set lead. Roddick was one set away from his first major victory.

Roddick started the third set with an easy service game that featured two aces and two brilliantly played shots at the net. In the longest game of the match, Ferrero prevailed on his first service game of the third set despite two deuces. On Roddick's next service game, he rushed to a 40-0 lead. Ferrero managed to get the next two point with one point gathered when Ferrero faked that he was going to his right and Roddick tried to slip one past Ferrero's backhand. It went wide but Roddick ended the game on the next serve as he won a long rally with Ferrero hitting the last return into the net.

Ferrero managed to get a 0-30 lead on Roddick's next service game but one ace and three out returns later, Roddick pulled out the game. After five games, the third set was on serve with Roddick ahead 3 games to 2.

Roddick's, on Ferrero's next service game had two breakpoints. Ferrero, down 15-40, needed the next two points to stay on serve. In one long rally, Ferrero floated a nice drop shot after a series of hard returns. Ferrero survived three break points to stay in the set.

On Roddick's next service game, it was Ferrero with a two break point advantage. Roddick eliminated the first with a nasty serve that Ferrero sent into the net. The next Ferrero return went into the stands as the Roddick serve went low. Roddick broke Ferrero only for the second time of the match as Ferrero double faulted, and this put Roddick in the driver's seat. With the set now 5 games to three, Roddick was one game away from the Open championship. The Roddick serve went into over drive as he closed the show with three straight aces. Roddick broke through for his first majors and the torch was finally passed from the Sampras-Agassi generation to a new generation of American Tennis stars led by Andy Roddick.

It was Roddick's power that prevailed over the crafty and speedy Spaniard, Ferrero. Ferrero was only broken twice but could not figure out how to defuse the power that was coming at him. It was not that Ferrero played poorly, it was that Roddick put his entire package together from the serve to his improved return and net play. There were times when Roddick looked like Sampras as he scored on 83% of his net games. The power of Roddick wore down Ferrero, who had to beat two former champions in the previous two days. After the match, Ferrero stated, "Today I didn't play my best tennis, but Andy played so good, and he served unbelievable, and I couldn't do much." As for Roddick, he merely said, "It hasn't sunk in…I came to this tournament so many times as a little kid and watched from way up there. I just can't believe it."

As the majors season ended, it became obvious a new generation of stars had moved forward to take their rightful place. Andre Agassi began the year by dominating the Australian Open in easy fashion, showing that the old lion still was one of the best, if not the best. For the early part of the Tennis season, Agassi was the number one rated player and at one time, fashioned an 18-1 record. Throughout the year, Agassi would be in the hunt for a major but it was the new generation of stars that took hold in the end. Juan Carlos Ferrero was considered the best on clay, but before 2003, he had yet to win the official clay championship—the French Open. Then this year, the young Spaniard finally punched through and won his major. Roger Federer was another young gun that everyone wanted to win a major. Pete Sampras, who lost to Federer in the 2002 Wimbledon, predicted that before this year's Wimbledon that Federer would win, and he did. Federer made his breakthrough, and now it was Andy Roddick who shredded the label of potential as he won the US Open. When Ferrero beat Agassi in the semis of the US Open, it signaled that the new generation had taken hold of the Tennis world and Roddick's victory demonstrated that for the next decade, new international rivalries would be developed.

As for Roddick, he had won six titles and this was his third title in a row. What lay ahead for Roddick was the conclusion of the Masters series, the Davis Cup and finally, the Masters Cup in Houston. About the US Open and the passing of the torch in American Tennis, Roddick said, "I don't think you could have written a script any better, you know. Starting it off with Pete's retirement, Chang is gone. All that. Its just—it was just too good."

5

Going For Number One and The Masters Cup

Part One: Davis Cup: Getting Back to the Sweet 16

Now that Andy Roddick conquered the world in New York for his first US Open, it was time for Roddick to lead the U.S. back into the upper elites of the Davis Cup. After their loss earlier this year, the United States lost to Croatia and now had to win just to get back in the hunt for 2004. Lose and they would have to re-qualify for 2005.

The United States-Slovakia Davis Cup match was the perfect test for the young Americans, who now had all their young guns ready to play. Mardy Fish had an excellent summer and James Blake was blessed with Davis Cup experience providing the United States with depth. The Bryan brothers were one of the World's best doubles teams and had shown an ability to win on Clay, the surface that the Americans were scheduled to play on.

The Slovaks had some excellent players of their own including Karol Kucera, who gave Roddick a tough match in the Canada Masters. As Roddick said, "I had a very tough match with Kucera in I think Montreal this year. He was up a break in the first set and I had to win the first set in a tie-break to win."

American captain Patrick McEnroe added, "We are expecting a tough match but we are confident. We know that the Slovaks have a lot of experience, especially in Davis Cup and we certainly are not expecting it to be easy, but we are extremely confident of our chances." About his young Americans, McEnroe concluded, "Playing away in Davis Cup is always tough but on the whole, our guys are playing the best they've ever played in their careers so that gives us a lot of confidence."

Slovakian Tennis star Karol Kucera told reporters, "I played against both Roddick and Fish recently, and so it was great to see them both play to get to know their game. I also know Blake. I also practiced with him on the clay court. The clay match now will be very different from the hard court game." Both teams were ready and while the Americans were favored because of Roddick, the clay surface could prove to be the great equalizer against the American power game.

In Roddick's first set, it appeared that the clay surface would prove no hindrance. Roddick's serve was on target as he easily held serve with seven aces. Up by 4 games to 3, Roddick managed to break Dominik Hrbaty and only spent 23 minutes winning the first set. It looked like an easy victory was within reach and Roddick easily picked up where he left off from his torrid summer.

The second set proved to be different. Hrbaty began to return Roddick's serves and managed to put the ball in play. The confidence that Roddick exuded in the first set soon eluded him. Hrbaty, using the clay as his launching pad, started to take control of the match. Hrbaty's groundstrokes frustrated Roddick; whose serve deserted him as well. Hrabty tied the match at one set apiece.

Suddenly what appeared an easy victory for the Americans was in doubt. Roddick certainly felt that he could turn it around as the third set began. In the third game, Hrabty broke Roddick again and took a 2 games to 1 lead with a service break. Hrabty was in control of the set. Roddick took his next service game. As the set progressed, so did Hrabty's confidence. He had already broken Roddick twice in the match, and now in the seventh game, he pushed Roddick to the limit on his service game. Hrabty took the game to deuce and threatened Roddick with yet another service break. Roddick went back to work but Hrabty's net play broke Roddick and Hrabty was now ahead 5 games to 2. Roddick salvaged a service break and was one service break from sending the set into a tiebreaker. In the next game, Roddick saved four match points in the final game of the set before succumbing to Hrabty.

Now down two sets to one, Roddick needed yet another miracle to save the first match for the Americans. Hrabty took command with a service game break in the second game. Roddick's frustration showed when he smashed his tennis racket with his foot. Both men held their next five-service game. The score was now 5 games to 4. Roddick hopes to send this set into a tiebreaker and move the match into a fifth set now came down to breaking Hrabty's service game. Roddick and Hrabty battled from the baseline as both men were knotted up at 30-30. Hrabty's excellent groundstrokes aimed at Roddick's backhand, ended the game, the set and the match. The Americans were one match down.

The upset put American Davis Cup hopes in Mardy Fish's hands. In the second set, Fish staved off set points and came back to win the set and later ended the match with a 6-1 last set. The series was tied at 1 match apiece and now it was up to the Bryan brothers to win the doubles match the next day. What was supposed to be a two match lead for the Americans with their anchor leading the way was now a nail biter with the Americans chance to join the top 16 in doubt.

After the match, Hrbaty said, "Roddick was not playing very well. He didn't play his best. But he's only a man of flesh and blood." Hrbaty quipped, "I hope we will show the Americans where the small nation of Slovakia is."

The Bryan brothers were the number one ranked doubles team and Patrick McEnroe brought the brothers in for one reason—their doubles expertise. Playing doubles is not the same as playing singles for two players must play as one. The Bryan twins were essentially one person operating seamlessly together, and their opponents, Karol Beck and Dominik Hrbaty rarely played doubles together. The Twins started off fast as they marched through the first set 6-1 and dominated the second as well 6-4. Against the Croatians, the Americans also had a 2 set lead but this was different. The Bryan brothers were the doubles specialists and now they had to close the show. The Slovak team forced a tiebreaker and had one opportunity to turn the match around. The tiebreaker was close but the Bryan brothers came through with a 7-5 win.

Now the Americans were one match away from winning the Davis Cup with Roddick coming back on Sunday against Kucera, the Slovaks number one player. While Roddick was the heavy favorite, and certainly Mardy Fish would be the favorite over Hrbaty, nothing could be certain. The clay surface would be a factor and Roddick had already lost, so Kucera had confidence going into the last day.

The next day saw a change in the Slovak game plan. Slovak captain Miloslav Mecir switched Karol Beck in place of Karol Kucera. Kucera was suffering from hamstring problems and Beck, who the day before lost in doubles, now confronted the American number one player. After the match, Kucera told reporters, "I was hoping during Saturday it would get better. I was trying to warm up and I kept feeling pain." The one saving grace in Beck's favor was that Roddick had lost three Davis Cup matches in a row, all on Clay.

Roddick had the chance to clinch the victory for the Americans. This was the moment that Roddick waited for, for victory meant that the United States was back in the final sixteen. Before the match, Patrick McEnroe commented, "I think he's going to be a different player. He's in a much better frame of mind." McEnroe was confident that Roddick was over his opening day loss and with Beck on board, this gave Roddick an added advantage.

Roddick was more confident, talking to himself and jawing with his teammates on the sideline. Roddick nailed six aces in the first set and Beck was consistently on his back foot as the powerful Roddick serve was hitting its mark. Beck's only counter in the first set was his drop shots. Roddick's groundstrokes errors kept the first set close though Roddick breezed through 6-3. Just like during his first match, Roddick went through his first set easily. Beck offered more resistance though and tried to turn the tide against Roddick. Roddick's groundstrokes allowed him to break Beck in the first game of the set. Beck broke Roddick back in the fourth game to put the set back on serve, and Roddick took command of the set with yet another service break in the fifth game as he took a 3 to 2 lead. The Roddick serve took over again as he won the set 6-4. Roddick added seven more aces to his total and now the Americans were one set from winning their section of the Davis Cup. One more set from being back in the top sixteen for the United States.

The key game was the fifth game of the set as Roddick broke Beck. He nailed a cross-court winner to get within one point of the game and then shot home one more winner down the line shouting for joy. Now he was in command and three more games from the match and the Davis Cup.

In the ninth game, he had a chance to end it with a match point but Beck saved it and now it was the tenth game and he was one service game away from the match. His service game was clicking and on the last point of the game, Beck struck a backhand wide. The Americans clinched the Davis Cup with one match left.

McEnroe's strategy paid off. With Roddick holding the anchor spot and the Bryan Brothers playing doubles, McEnroe had the team primed for the competition. The key acquisition was the Bryan Brothers and Mardy Fish as they made up for Roddick's opening upset. The Bryan Brothers seamless play in their doubles and Mardy Fish's gritty play set the stage for the victory with Roddick finishing the show. After the match, Roddick said, "I just came here knowing it was one match to go and I wanted to close it out. I would have felt pretty bad if I lost again…the team stepped up this time." Roddick was definitely acting like the anchor to the American Davis Cup.

Roddick added, "I wanted to come out there with a lot of energy. I tried to play that first match like I played all summer—calm, cool and collected. But I think the Davis Cup is a totally different scenario. If you're feeling it, you've got to be jazzed."

The match did have its own price tag for Roddick. Roddick was forced to withdraw from the Thailand Open due to a Hamstring strain. The withdrawal cost Roddick $40,000 in fines and he was forced to forfeit the appearance money provided by the promoters. Weller Evans, ATP executive vice president of players' services quipped, "Obviously, everybody is disappointed that Andy will not be participating—with the possible exception of the other players."

As for the Americans, it was back to the sweet 16 and another crack at the Davis Cup. In 2004, they would be playing once again for the Davis Cup.

Part Two: Roddick at the Madrid Masters

After suffering from strained hamstrings and taking off a month after the US Open, Roddick began the final push toward the Houston Masters Cup. From this point forward, Roddick faced competition from J.C. Ferrero and Roger Federer in the race to see who would be best Tennis player for 2003. The first stop was the Madrid Masters with his first opponent at the Madrid Masters Max Mirnyi, alias the Beast.

The first set seemed as if Roddick had never left the courts for a month. In just 26 minutes, Roddick rolled Mirnyi over. Breaking Mirnyi's serve in the first game, Roddick sailed through the rest of the set. Mirnyi lost two more service breaks and the set ended 6-1.

The second set was different. Max Mirnyi found his rhythm in his serve and both men held their service game. The second set ended in a tiebreaker. In the tiebreak, Roddick had two opportunities to end the match when he had match point at 7-6 and 9-8 before losing the second set in a tiebreak.

Roddick was holding his serve and Max Mirnyi was in the position of playing the perfect game. Throughout the entire match, Roddick's service game was dominant, as he didn't lose one service game. Mirnyi matched Roddick serve for serve until the 11th game. With the eleventh game on the line, Roddick nailed a vicious return that Miryni returned back into the net. Roddick secured the match as he served out the next game.

Roddick's next opponent was Chilean Nicolas Massu. Previously, Massu defeated Gustavo Kuerten and now had Roddick in his sights. As for Roddick, the last time he lost an ATP event was the seminfinals in the Washington D.C. event last August. The only other loss was when Dominik Hrbaty upset Roddick in the Davis Cup after the US Open. Roddick was now the number one target for the other players on the tour.

Roddick started out this match as he did the previous match when he went up 5-2. In the sixth game, Roddick broke Massu to take a 4 game to 2 lead and after defending his serve, he appeared to be on the way to easily winning the set. The ninth game changed the momentum as Massu turned the tables and broke Roddick. This set up a tiebreaker as both men defended their service game for the rest of the set.

Massu, who had only lost 5 tiebreakers in 19 previous attempts, fell behind 3-2 and it appeared once again that Roddick would prevail. Massu, pressuring Roddick throughout the second half of the set, won the next five points in a miniature blitzkrieg. Massu won the opening set and Roddick felt the effects.

After defending his service game at the beginning of the second set, Massu broke Roddick for a second time as he took a two games to nothing lead. Massu turned the tables on the master server, as his next two service games were love affairs with Massu taking all the points. The final nail in the coffin came in the eighth game as Massu broke Roddick's service game one more time. Roddick double-faulted in this game and Massu had his second upset victory in a row.

After the match, Massu said, "The tennis I played today was incredible." Massu added, "In the first four, five games I was a little bit tight. After he broke me, I changed my game a little bit. I started feeling better. When I was down 5-2, I had no pressure because I thought I had lost the set. When I broke him I got a lot of confidence."

In the post match interview, Roddick said, "He played a great match. I played a bad game at 5-3 to let him into it. From then on he just played really good tennis. On the first tiebreaker, I played pretty well up to 4-3. A couple of points I thought I had him, and he came up with shots that were too good."

For Massu, this was his biggest victory on the tour. For Roddick, it was a hangover from the U.S.Open and the recovery from his pulled hamstring. Even with the defeat, Roddick was still in good shape in the championship race. He was still in the hunt for the elusive number one ranking.

Part Three: Roddick plays at Basel

After a quick exit at the Madrid Masters, Roddick headed toward Basel, Switzerland for the Basel Open. His first opponent was qualifier Jean Claude Scherrer. Staying in what Roddick described as the oldest hotel in Europe, the Roddick camp had a kind of looseness about them. (Roddick quipped that Napoleon supposedly once stayed in their hotel and joked that his coach was recovering from bad shins from walking into the bed the night before.)

Roddick wrote for his website, "Practices have been going great since we arrived here from Madrid. Things definitely could have gone better in Madrid, but losing, unfortunately, is part of sports."

His first match versus Jean-Claude Scherrer began in easy fashion as Roddick took the first set 6-3. The second set proved different as Roddick fell behind to the 291st ranked player 3 games to zero. Scherrer was within a point of taking an 4 games to 1 lead before Roddick held off the onslaught and turned it around. Roddick forced the set into a tiebreaker before prevailing 7-4. After the match, Roddick told reporters, "I figured it would be one of two situations. Either he would get really scared by the situation, facing a Top 10 (player) on center court, or he would play with nothing to lose. I think it was a little of the latter tonight."

In his second match, Roddick found himself fighting power failures as well as his opponent, qualifier Gilles Elseneer. Twice play was interrupted for 20 minutes as the lights went out in the indoor arena. Not that it helped Elseneer much in the first set. After playing Roddick even for the seven games, Elseneer was broken in the in the eighth game and fell behind 5 games to 3. Roddick closed the show in the final game and took the first set 6-3.

Elseneer took the first three game of the second set and appeared ready to even the match. Roddick slowly crawled back in the match and broke Elseneer's serve in the ninth game to put the set back on serve. Both men traded service games the rest of the set and the second set ended up in a tiebreaker. The tiebreaker was tight before Roddick sent a blistering ace to tie the extra set at 5 apiece. Roddick finished up the next two points and prevailed in the tiebreak 7-5. As Roddick prepared for his next opponent, Olivier Rochus, Roger Federer was upset by Ivan Ljubicic. Federer lost in his own backyard and Roddick was now the favorite to take his seventh title of the year.

Roddick's match with Rochus was his easiest. He broke Rochus once in each set, which was all he needed as he swept through Rochus on his service games. While Roddick was defeating Rochus, David Nalbandian was brushing off Tim Henman 6-2, 6-4. These men were meeting for the first time since their classic match in the US Open semifinals. Not only that, but a victory over Nalbandian would give Roddick the number one ranking in the championship race. After the Rochus match, Roddick said, "I still have a lot of work to do. I'm unfortunately not going to seal the deal here in Basel. My goal was to make the Masters Cup this year, I've accomplished more than that." Roddick added that David Nalbandian has "been the best player so far in this tournament. We definitely had a couple of tough matches. It's going to be a battle. I have to play well if I want to win. I think it'll be a good match." Roddick concluded, "Today I hit the ball the best so far. My mind was right. I was into it. It was a good game." About the Henman match, Nalbandian said, "Today, I played very good. The first set was almost perfect. He started to serve a little bit better in the second set, but one break was enough for me."

Nalbandian had revenge on his mind as Roddick had denied him his chance to reach the US Open finals. Nalbandian started off by breaking Roddick at the beginning and took a quick 3 games to 1 lead. Roddick came back as he broke Nalbandian in the 10th game, and all the memories of New York must have seeped back into Nalbandian's mind. After falling behind Roddick 5 games to 4, Nalbandian took the next three games and broke Roddick once more while taking the first set.

The second set was a tight affair with both men holding serve until the eleventh game, when Nalbandian broke Roddick one more time. Nalbandian served out the final game and took the match 7-5, 7-5 and was now in the finals. Throughout the match, Nalbandian showed splendid tactical play and while Roddick serve was constantly in the high 130's, Nalbandian consistently showed why he was one of the best returners in the game as Roddick found himself chasing down the Argentinian's returns. Nalbandian was consistently shooting baseline shots past the young American.

To reporters after the match, Roddick said, "I'm not disappointed with my performance. He just played better." Roddick added, "I feel my form was better leaving Basel than when I arrived, I feel optimistic about the next couple of weeks." This victory strengthened Nalbandian's chance of making it to the Masters Cup with the Paris Masters coming up. Nalbandian confessed to reporters,

"It was a very tough match, but I tried to take my chance in the rallies from the baseline, and the one break in the second set was perfect for me."

Roddick served 13 aces but was only able to get 58% of his first serve in and this slowed down the Roddick express. His loss in the opening service game set the tone for the rest of the match. Nalbandian told one reporter, "Not bad," when asked how he felt beating Roddick for the first time in his career. As for Roddick, the Paris Masters and the Masters Cup offered the final two opportunities to finish number one for the year.

Part Four: Paris Masters

Roger Federer and J.C. Ferrero were locked in a battle to see who would finish number one for the year along with Roddick. With but a sliver separating these three combatants, every match appeared magnified. Roddick's first opponent was Romanian Victor Hanescu and this match was a tough one for Roddick. Hanescu played Roddick even, and Roddick was a break down, and two set points from losing the set, before coming back and forcing the first set into a tie-breaker. Roddick prevailed in the tiebreaker 7-4 and the second game was not much easier. With both men holding serve, Hanescu forced Roddick to a second tiebreaker with Roddick proving once again his power in the clutch as he won 7-4.

Roddick felt lucky as he told reporters, "I was lucky to even take the first set to a tiebreaker. He had a couple of set points but I scrapped, clawed around and hung in there."

Roddick faced Tommy Robredo in the third round of the Paris Masters and beat the young Spaniard in 62 minutes, 6-3, 6-4. Roddick dominated from the start of the match, and after the match Roddick found out that he held the number 1 ranking. He was now the youngest American since John McEnroe to hold the number 1 ranking. The J.C. Ferrero upset defeat at the hand of Czech player Jiri Novak handed Roddick the number one ranking. With Ferrero no longer number one, Roddick was given the opportunity to gain ground over Ferrero and Federer.

Summing up his competitive spirit, Roddick told reporters, "I've got to No. 1 and no one can ever take that away from me. But I like to be greedy and I want to stay there for a long time."

Roddick became the sixth American to hold the number ranking since ATP began the ranking systems in 1973. Roddick added, "It's almost been scripted with Ferrero winning on clay (French Open), Roger Federer on grass (Wimbledon) and me at the U.S. Open. All of us were thinking at the start of the year 'when's our time gonna' come?" While Roddick was basking in the glory of reaching the number one ranking, he still had to play Sweden's Jonas Bjorkman.

Andy Roddick and Jonas Bjorkman played a tight, tough match. Both men stayed on serve until the eleventh game when Roddick finally broke Bjorkman and then closed out the set 7-5. Bjorkman stayed even with Roddick in the second set, with both men breaking the other man's serve one time. The second set went to a tiebreaker, then Roddick cleaned house and easily won 7 zip, blanking the Swede to clinch one of the semifinal spots.

Tim Henman, in his last match with Roddick, lost in the opening round of the US Open. Henman now was in full stride and played a classic match against Roddick. Nip and Tuck, both sets went to tiebreaker. Henman took the first game of the first set and set the pace through out until the tenth game when Roddick broke Henman's service game and tied the set. The first tiebreaker ended with a Henman 7-4 victory as Henman's classic serve and volley game was working to perfection.

The second set saw each man hold his own service games and once again, Roddick and Henman played a tiebreaker. Henman began fast in the tiebreak but Roddick came back to tie 7-7. Henman held an 8-7 lead with match point. Roddick went for broke in an effort to tie the match but his forehand went wide. Henman went on to win the Paris Masters.

Part Five: The Masters Cup and the Final Drive for Number One

The final chapter of the 2003 season began in Houston as the top eight players matched up in a round robin tournament. Players are split into two groups, Red Group and Blue Group. Roddick was placed with Guillermo Coria, Rainer Schuettler, Carlos Moya whereas J.C. Ferrero, David Nalbandian, Roger Federer and Andre Agassi were in the Blue group. Susan Seemiller of Bob Larson Tennis wrote, "My overall impression of the Masters Cup is that it is underrated. To see the top players playing each other in this type of format guarantee some great matches, and we saw that."

The players competed against each other once with the top two from each group advancing to the semifinals, and the final two standing playing for the championship. Before Roddick played his first match against the seventh seed Carlos Moya, David Nalbandian surprised J.C. Ferrero, and Schuettler upset Coria. Federer and Agassi engaged in a tough three set which featured two tiebreakers. Federer triumphed over the veteran Agassi for the first time in his career.

Roddick and Moya were the final duo to compete in the first round. Roddick drew first blood as he broke Moya's serve in the third game and took an early 2 games to 1 lead in the first set. Roddick began that critical game with a beautiful cross—court winner off Moya's serve and ended the game in the same way. Roddick dominated the service game and his return game was working beautifully as he took the seventh game and a 5 to 2 lead. In the crucial seventh game, Moya felt the pressure as he went for broke. Moya's chances of winning the set were dashed when his last shot went wide and now Roddick had one more service game left to clinch the first set. Roddick concluded the first set not with his typical power serve but a beautiful drop shot as he rushed to the net. Roddick easily took the first set as he won 6-2. It only took 23 minutes.

The second set proved to be much different as Moya broke Roddick in the second game and rushed to a 3 games to zip lead before Roddick won his first service game of the set and kept the set close. Moya was mixing up crosscourt winners past Roddick when Roddick came to the net and had an excellent service game that was missing in the first set. This was Moya's set as he easily took the set 6 games to 3 and now the match would go to a third and final set.

Roddick opened the third set with an easy service game and both men held their service game till Roddick won the eighth game by breaking Moya and was now one game away from the match and his first victory in the Masters Cup. He concluded the match with an ace and service winner. Roddick was missing his first serve more than half of the time but did score 14 aces.

Moya told reporters, "His serve makes a big difference, and he can mix the game well, too. He can go to the net, he can stay at the baseline. He's playing very smart." When asked about how he felt after dropping the second set, Roddick responded, "Luckily, I was able to recover in time for the third set. I felt pretty good in the first set. In the second and third, he was dictating things with his forehand." Roddick added that the key to winning the third set was to hold on his serve, which he did.

Roddick's next opponent was Schuettler, who won his first match. Before Roddick set foot on the court to face Schuettler, Andre Agassi presented Roddick with a gift, a victory over J.C. Ferrero. This victory clinched the number one ranking for Roddick, who now became the sixth American to finish the year as the world's best.

Roddick played as if number one was still at stake. He won nine of the first 11 points and Schuettler was broken in the first game. Schuettler was frustrated as he made error after error and even swatted a ball into the stands after double faulting one of his serves.

Roddick and Schuettler traded breaks in the eight and ninth games and Roddick held an 5 games to 4 lead. Schuettler had a chance to break Roddick a second time in the tenth game as he had a break point over Roddick. Roddick nailed a forehand to bring the game to deuce and then kicked in an ace to take the advantage and took the set with a forehand winner.

Schuettler and Roddick protected their service game and the second set went into tiebreaker. Schuettler rushed to a 4 to 1 lead and took the first tiebreaker as Roddick's last forehand soared into the net.

In the last set, Roddick appeared to take control of the set as he broke Schuettler in the second game. After smacking a cross-court forehand to the corner, Roddick pumped his fist, and the fans shared Roddick's own confidence that he was on his way to the semi-finals. Schuettler broke Roddick in the fifth game and then from this point, Schuettler and Roddick defended their service game.

At the end of the match, Roddick's serve went south as he double-faulted six times in the final set. The match concluded with Roddick sending a backhand long to give Schuettler a victory in the second tiebreaker. Schuettler defeated Roddick for the third time in the past year and seemed to have Roddick's number in 2003. The first two victories were a result of injuries to Roddick but in this match; there were no excuses. Schuettler faced a healthy Roddick and still won in a tight three set match that included two tiebreakers. Schuettler made the big shots and now Roddick had to beat Guillermo Coria to gain entrance into the semi-finals.

After the match, Roddick expressed disappointment at losing and was humble about his number one ranking. Roddick told reporters, "If you look at the Americans who have finished No. 1, I don't put myself in that category. But I'm working on it." Susan Seemiller observed, "It was difficult for Andy today to accept the No. 1 trophy after that loss, but to be frank, both guys gave it their all out there in windy conditions, and they never stopped fighting. Rainer played the big points a bit better, and I think Andy lost concentration a few times. But both commented on the wind." She added, "He was not happy since he lost till Mardy Fish came in with champagne at the press conference." (Roddick's close friend, Mardy Fish, sneaked up on Roddick at Roddick's press conference and poured champagne over Andy. The two playfully wrestled each other and because of that stress reliever, Roddick seemed more relaxed throughout the rest of the press conference.)

ESPN Tennis commentator Malival Washington added, "What's remarkable is that halfway through the season, people were wondering if he could win a major. People were wondering if Roddick could move into the upper tier of players, a tier that includes Roger Federer, Lleyton Hewitt and Ferrero—players Roddick had never beaten before. He not only moved into that tier but also rose above them all." Roddick had now climbed to the top. Roddick, however, wanted more. He wanted to win the Masters Cup and now it was a do or die battle with Coria to see which one would reach the semi-finals.

Roddick won the first set 6-3 by serving it out as he managed to out hustle the Argentine. In the third game of the second set, Roddick broke Coria to gain the edge. In the fourth game, Roddick had an opportunity to put distance between him and Coria, but Coria broke Roddick's back and now the set was tied.

Roddick began the sixth game with three unreturnable serves and closed out the game to keep the set even. Coria began the next game with a forehand just out and Rodddick jumped out to a 0-30 lead on Coria next service game. Coria saved his sevice game by nailing the next four points and concluded with a nice drop shot. Coria appeared to be gaining confidence as the set wore on. In the first game, Roddick's service game was better, though now Coria was returning the Roddick serve and forcing the action. In the eighth game, Roddick saved break point and won by attacking the net.

Coria took the ninth game with combinations of forehands and drop shots. Roddick's service game warmed up as he tied the set with an ace. Coria ripped through Roddick in the eleventh game and now was one game from tying the match. Roddick opened the twelfth game with two unreturnable serves but Coria tied the game up with a forehand. Roddick sent the set into tiebreaker by taking the next two points.

Coria took the first three points of the tiebreaker and while Roddick broke Coria's next serve, Coria took control of the set by smashing a forehand winner and now had a 4-1 lead. Roddick took the next two points on his serve and now it was 4-3 with Coria serving. Coria's drop shot moved the score ahead 5-3. Coria scored with yet another drop shot and, with a 6-3 lead, he was three-break points away from victory. Roddick double faulted to end the tiebreaker and Coria won the set. Roddick failed to take advantage of his break in the third game and Coria dominated the tiebreaker.

Going into the third set, Roddick had nearly tripled the unforced errors over Coria. The third set began with Coria scoring on the first two Roddick serves and Coria forcing long rallies. Coria, using a tough forehand and wicked backhand, won the opening game of the set. Coria won his next service game as he took four of the five points. Roddick saved the next game with his serve but Coria moved closer to taking the match as Roddick's back hand hit the net and Coria now led 3 games to one. After defending his service game, Roddick broke Coria by scoring four straight points after Coria took the first two points of the game. Coria's forehand landed in the net and now the set was tied. Roddick nailed four straight serves and now he took the lead at 4 games to three.

Roddick now went for the knock out blow as he started to return Coria's serve. Coria's shots were stopping at the net in the crucial eighth game, and Roddick was now one game from the match. Roddick's service game kicked into higher gear as he marched into the semifinals with an ace down the middle.

Roddick-Federer followed the Agassi-Schuettler match in which Agassi moved toward the finals, just waiting for the winner of the Roddick-Federer match.

Federer's smooth style vs. the power game of Roddick was the underlying theme of this match. Roger Federer had the complete game but Roddick's power could change the tenor of the game. The first set opened up as both men held their service game. Roddick was hitting 70% of his first serve and this allowed him to hold his service game whereas Federer's smooth game allowed the Swiss to maintain control of his serve. Roddick would torque his body around when delivering his massive forehand at Federer. Federer, on the other hand, looked flawless, as he threw off combinations of drop shots and forehand. Federer's control of angles was forcing Roddick on his heels throughout the match.

The first set ended in a tiebreak. Federer took the first point and this set the stage for the tiebreaker. Roddick looked frustrated as he could get nothing past Federer and Federer played with a rhythm that seemed effortless. Federer easily took the tiebreaker 7-2 and this set the trend for the next set. The second set began just as the first with both men defending the service game, though Roger Federer seemed to be holding his game more confidently than Andy. The fifth game of the second set, that confidence led to the first service break as Federer broke Roddick. Federer pushed one-handed backhand shots past Roddick, who could hardly believe the accuracy of Federer's returns.

When Federer broke Roddick in the fifth game for the first time, the match was effectively over. Federer took the next three games as he played flawless tennis. On this night, no one could have beaten Federer as he played the way he had in Wimbledon. Federer defeated Roddick for the fifth time in six matches.

After the match, Roddick said, "Federer doesn't really have any big weaknesses—especially when he serves the way he did tonight. His percentage had to be up close to 65, 70 percent. It definitely makes the job tough." After the match, Susan Seemiller said, "Well, the first set was a serving display—not the most exciting tennis, but it was something to see Andy being out-Andied—not being able to get a look at a ball. Still, a tiebreak seemed inevitable, and I was surprised that Roger took it so easily." She added that after the first Agassi match on Monday, "Federer started to play at a different level than others." And this was demonstrated emphatically when Federer easily dispatched Agassi in three straight sets in the final the next day.

On this night, art beat power as Roddick could not overpower the crafty Swiss, though for many tennis pundits, there was a general feeling this was part of Tennis's future. The Roddick-Federer rivalry had the potential of matching those of McEnroe-Borg or Sampras-Agassi. On this evening, the Swiss was the victorious one playing like he was the best in the world. Roddick, after the match, must have felt that he had seen the future and it was not pretty or easy. For Roddick, the gauntlet was put down; for to defend his number one ranking, he must figure out how to master the suave Swiss. Roddick now had his challenge for 2004.

But what a season!! Roddick's goal was to make it to the Masters Cup and he exceeded his own expectations. He won his first major and finished the season as the number one player. He came of age.

6

Summary

Part One: Andy on the Difficulty of Tennis

What is the most difficult thing in Sports? Ted Williams often stated it was hitting a baseball. With a small sphere hurtling along at 90 to100 mph in your direction, you have less than one third of a second to react. Less than one third of a second to decide whether you are swinging at a strike or a ball. One third of a second is close to the blink of an eye, and yet it is the difference between striking out or hitting the game winning home run.

Hockey purists would argue it is being a goalie with a puck that travels up to 100 mph with you standing in its path. Of course, putting a hockey puck in the net may be even more difficult. The average goalie will save 90% of all shots coming in their direction.

NFL quarterbacks will hit close to 60% of their passes and if anything, it has become easier to throw a football over the past four decades. Bobby Layne was a hall of fame quarterback while completing less than half of his passes. After the 1970's, the NFL has changed the rules that penalized the defense while aiding and, even in some cases, inflating NFL quarterback statistics.

Boxing is another sport that ranks as one of the hardest in my own estimation. Sugar Ray Leonard told of how he invited Marcus Allen to hit the heavy bag for three minutes and Marcus could only finish two minutes. "Throw in a foe who hits you back," Sugar Ray said, "and that makes boxing the most difficult in the world."

So how does Tennis rate in the difficulty debate? Andy Roddick has one of the hardest serves and when asked by Gary Mihoces of USA TODAY how difficult it was to return a 130 mph serve, Roddick replied, "I'd say it's pretty high up there on the list. Being able to return a serve at that speed is one of the biggest things that separates the professionals from the recreational players. It's not just about the power. There are different spins and placements, so pure speed is only one of your worries."

Just like a baseball moving in different directions on its way from the pitcher to the batter, a tennis ball will move as well. A player not only has to defend against the serve, he has to anticipate where the ball is going and react to that. "If you watch the best players, placement can be as deadly as speed," Roddick said, "At the pro level, serving is as much about tactics as power." Andre Agassi is a baseline counter puncher and is considered one of the best returners in the game. His serve rarely goes beyond 100 mph but he is expert at placing his serve where his opponent is not.

"Probably the most important thing is to stay quick mentally," Roddick said, "If you get discouraged and your mind starts to wander, then the serves start flying past you." Often in a Tennis game, concentration can wander after an hour of play has past. "It helps to have a short memory. You have to be able to brush off a bad loss to compete the next week," Roddick said, "It's similar with a big serve. You have to be able to focus on everyone, so you can't get down about the one that gets away from you." Just like a baseball hitter, a Tennis player needs a short memory. A baseball hitter will only succeed 3 out of 10 times, if he is good. And he will bat over 500 times in a season. A Tennis player will serve anywhere from 150 to 200 serves in a match. He will return a similar amount so there is no luxury in mulling over a previous shot.

When Pete Sampras played Andre Agassi in the 2001 U.S. Open quarterfinals, he scored about 80% of his serves that were in play. Sampras did not lose a service game and Agassi is one of the best returners.

Howard Brody, a retired professor of physics believes that 130 mph serves are pushing the limit of a human's ability to return the ball. Air resistance and friction of the bounce slows the ball and gives returners a chance to counterpunch back. A tennis player has less than half of a second to return a serve, and as Mr. Brody observed, that good returners "have incredibly good eye sight."

The fuzz on the tennis ball slows the serve but enables the server to put a topspin on the ball. Andy Roddick has recorded one of the fastest serves at last year's US Open, and his ability to smash the monster serve gives him an advantage. The average serve is 115 mph and a second serve may go on an average of 103 mph, so Andy Roddick's serve is over 20 mph faster than the average Tennis player. While Andy acknowledges the difficulty of returning serves, it could be said that it is even more difficult to return a Roddick serve. Clyde Dexler, the NBA great, commented, "Roddick's serve whistling by your ear feels like a 747 rushing by." Dexler made his comments after playing in a charity exhibition match as Andy's teammate.

Part Two: The Art of the Double Play

Doubles represents a different aspect of Tennis. The key is to coordinate your game plan to swat at a ball that is traveling 100 mph. Each player on each point has a role and the key is to cover specific zones. Andy Roddick and Mardy Fish in their opening match at the Houston Clay championship against Sebastian Prieto and Andre Sa demonstrated how a doubles-team focuses as a team. In their 6-1, 6-2 victory, the Roddick-Fish team showed doubles at its best.

Doubles does not necessarily belong to the best, but to those two individuals who can synchronize their attack. Often, double-matches represents trench warfare at the net with the rackets representing weapons, and the ball representing the ammunition. The key is to direct the ball through holes in the other team's defenses. While the outside line is added, the court is essentially cut in half between the two defenders. Reporter Brad Falkner of Tennis Week told me, "first off, I believe that strong chemistry between the partners is the essential ingredient. In other words, the pair must be supportive of one another and able to communicate well with each other." Falkner added, "Both must possess more than adequate volley skills. Moreover the ability at the net is an important key."

Good serving and returning are paramount to success and as Falkner added, "who plays what side of the court is very relevant." A successful doubles team is a perfect marriage of two skilled professionals, and in an era when doubles is being de-emphasized, we may see even less of the great doubles teams. For many players, doubles is a way to stay in Tennis longer but as Tennis seeks higher ratings, doubles is slowly being laid aside. For TV, it is the singles matches that make ratings and drama. Except for the hardcore Tennis fan, who understands the intricacies of the game, most fans are ambivalent toward doubles. While the average Sunday hacker will play doubles, they are more interested in watching the singles players. The ATP has slashed prize money and draw sizes for doubles in most tournaments. Houston, was one of the few events that had a full doubles draw. Most tournaments it's size have cut it down to 16 teams. Unless a top player is involved, doubles usually do not produce much in excitement or ratings and that is premier in the minds of TV executives. Doubles however is a game of skill and teamwork. One of the world's best is the Bryan twins, who play doubles as if they are one. For one brief match, Roddick and Fish showed how to play doubles.

Part Three—The Standard of American Tennis

There have been many great players in American Men's Tennis but American Tennis is defined by the following men: Bill Tilden, Don Budge, Tony Trabert, Arthur Ashe, Jimmy Connors, John McEnroe, Pete Sampras and Andre Agassi. These are the legends of American Tennis and the men that all are measured by includes Andy Roddick. When Roddick finishes his career, he will be compared to these greats in the past.

As for American players, three out of the top four most successful players as measured by overall singles titles in the open arena were Americans. If you want to count Ivan Lendl, a Czechoslovakian player who became an American citizen, then Americans occupy the first four.

The 1920's were the golden era of sports when sports figures were not just athletes but mythical gods. Babe Ruth, Jack Dempsey, Bobby Jones, Red Grange, and **Bill Tilden**, these men were the stuff of legends. Their exploits were reported in newspapers and broadcast on radio, though most sports fans never saw their heroes live. The era of television in some ways has removed the mythical status as even the most spectacular plays become the routine as they are shown over and over and over again on ESPN or other 24 hour news outlets. To listen to a event on radio, you must allow your imagination to go and sports writers in the 20's did not report, but instead mythologized their sports figures. A Babe Ruth or Bill Tilden performance was recorded in the same way as were major historical events with sports writers creating legends.

In the 1920's **Bill Tilden** was Tennis. This was a man who quit going to Wimbledon for a period of four years because he did not think it was worth the effort to take a boat across the Atlantic just to record an easy victory. Tilden was never lacking for confidence. Tilden made the US Open his personal playpen and in the 1920's, the Davis Cup stayed in the United States with Tilden routinely leading the United States to victory.

Like Jack Dempsey and Babe Ruth, Tilden would stride onto a Tennis Court as if it was a mere prop in a Broadway play, with his opponent often playing the supporting role in his drama. For six straight years, he won every major title that he entered, including six U.S. Nationals between 1920 and 1925. Tilden was as much an actor as an athlete, and his legend was formed from word of mouth with his exploits exaggerated and given supernatural components.

Bill Tilden was born in prosperity and never loved Tennis as a young man. His mother protected him excessively, and he was not even allowed to go to the city parks as a youth. His mother was forever giving him lectures about young women and venereal disease. Tilden was sheltered from life in his formative years. He was a latecomer when it came to being a championship Tennis player. It was not until he reached 27 years of age before he finally won his first championship, though after that he was unbeatable.

In 1919, Tilden would lose to Bill Johnston at the US Open as Johnston took advantage of Tilden's weak backhand. Tilden spent the next year working on his backhand. He convinced a wealthy executive that he would coach the executive's son on tennis if he could practice his Tennis on the executive's indoor Tennis Court. This practice changed Tilden and from that point on, Tilden dominated Tennis the way Babe Ruth dominated baseball and Bobby Jones dominated Golf. Tilden developed a topspin backhand after chopping wood daily to gain strength. He revenged his previous loss to Bill Johnston in the 1920 Open, and from that point on, Tilden became synonymous with American Tennis.

Tilden loved Broadway and invested in many plays, though unfortunately, many of his investments went sour. Tilden was a genius on the court but not necessarily off the court. Like many great athletes, he could be cocky but he did turn a nation on to Tennis. It was not until the late 60's that professional players would be allowed in the majors and Tilden did not start playing professional until 1930 when he was close to 40 years of age. Between 1931 and 1937, Tilden earned $500,000, but as he become older, his game deteriorated. He also became more open with his homosexuality, which cost him matches and income. He escorted teenage boys to clubs, and many Tennis clubs would ban him as a result.

After World War II, he was arrested for having fondled and making unwanted advances to teenage boys on two different occasions but his sexual peccadilloes did not deny Tilden his place on Tennis's Olympus. It did hurt his ability to earn income and when he died in 1953, he died penniless. Tilden today is remembered less for his lifestyle but more for his artistry on the Tennis Court. He was Tennis's first superstar, and set a standard for both skills and flamboyance. Not even a young Agassi could compete with the master showman, "Big Bill Tilden."

In1937 and 1938, **Don Budge** dominated the Tennis world as no one had since Bill Tilden, and no American would ever match. With a booming serve and stylish backhand, Don Budge stood 6'1" and towered over the Tennis court. Budge's most notable achievement was becoming the first player to win the grand slam in one season. In 1938, he would win the Australian, French and United States national championships plus Wimbledon.

Budge's coming out party was the previous year. In 1936, Budge lost to Fred Perry in two close matches in the US Open and Wimbledon. Perry became a professional the next year, leaving Budge the opportunity to take control of the amateur Tennis world. (Until the late 1960's, only amateurs were allowed to play in Tennis tournaments including the majors. For many fine players, the professional route was the only way to earn money but it denied them their chance of immortality.)

Budge's official coming out party was in 1937 at Wimbledon where he was victorious over Baron Von Cramm in straight sets. Then Budge would engage in one of the greatest Tennis games ever played with Baron Von Cramm in the Davis Cup interzone play. Von Cramm was up two sets to zero, and rushed to a 4-1 lead in the third set. The end was near. Budge came back to win the third set and took the fourth set. In the final set, both men waged a life and death game as the score remained tied after the twelfth game. Budge took the thirteenth game and had a 7-6 lead. In those days, there were no tiebreakers so Budge faced a longer contest. He managed to edge the German though winning one of Tennis's great comebacks as America defeated Germany. Later that year, Budge would single handedly defeat Great Britain and lead the United States to a Davis Cup. This was America's first Davis Cup in eleven years since the days of Big Bill Tilden.

1938 was the year that Budge made history. He swept through the majors and after that year decided to go professional. At the age of 23, Budge would no longer chase the majors cups, and there is no telling how many titles he would have won if he had continued to play the circuit. Tennis fans would have to wait until the 1970's before they were treated to the best players participating in the majors who were forgoing the "professional circuit."

In 1937, Budge was the winner of the James Sullivan trophy for best amateur athlete, and the next year he would win the Associated Press athlete of the year. No American dominated Tennis the way Budge did in 1938 and, not since Tilden had any American dominated Tennis the way Budge did for that one season. Nor would any American since have the kind of season that Budge did. Not Sampras, not Agassi, not Trabert. For one season, Budge was the greatest.

Tony Trabert was the All-American kid with a nice crew cut and a scientific touch for the game. Hailing from Cincinnati, Trabert learned his game from Bill Talbert, a great doubles player. Trabert practiced and conditioned himself while learning how to play the angles and subtleties of tactics.

Between 1953 and 1955, Trabert took 2 US Opens, 2 French Opens and one Wimbledon. No American would win the French Open till Michael Chang in 1989, ending a 35-year drought.

Like many talented players, Trabert turned pro after 1955. Trabert won 17 straight tournaments in 1955 and it was evident that he was head and shoulders above his fellow amateurs, so there was only one option left. Make money by playing professional tennis. Again, like Budge and Perry before him, Trabert left the tournament circuit while hitting his prime. Like Budge and Perry, we will never know what further impact Trabert would have had on the history of Tennis. The absurdity of allowing only "amateurs" to play Tennis denied Tennis fans the chance to see the greatest play. Trabert would play the professional circuit for eight years and then later ran the professional tour as well.

Arthur Ashe won three majors. Jim Courier won four majors. Arthur Ashe is an historical figure whereas Jim Courier is a good player who played in the shadow of Sampras and Agassi. So why include Ashe as one of America's greats? Simple, Ashe was the first African-American male tennis star and his accomplishments go beyond the tennis court.

Ashe was a thoughtful man off the court, and was an activist for civil rights and later for AIDS research, a disease he eventually died from. An author of African-American athletic history, Ashe was more than a Tennis player; he was an historian as well.

On the court, Ashe played an audacious game full of risk. He would do running backhand passing toss, go for broke on second serves and angled volleys in the corner. When he was on, he could march through a tournament like the 1968 US Open. When the bold risk failed, Ashe played the bridesmaid. As Ashe got older, he reigned himself in and played a more disciplined game. 1975 was his best year, capped by his victory over the young Jimmy Connors at Wimbledon. He varied his pace and spins as he showed patience against the young and rising star, marching to an easy upset victory.

Ashe was a thinly built player with great wrist action but what distinguished him most was his knowledge of the game, which allowed him to beat more talented players. His Wimbledon victory was a victory of brains over brawn and talent. Ashe always had the pressure of "representing" his race for when Ashe played, the civil rights act was in full bloom and racism was stronger that it is today. He conducted clinics for underprivileged kids and when he went to South Africa in 1973—it was not because he was a pawn of White racist South Africa as some would claim, but to learn more about the system. For Ashe, the benefits of seeing a black man of accomplishment was important for young black South Africans to observe.

Growing up in Richmond, the capital of the old Confederacy, Ashe saw racism on a daily basis. For Ashe, being black in America was challenge enough and as a 15 year-old tennis player, he was denied access to a movie theater after a tournament due to his race. Ashe would spend three years writing a book on the history of black athletes in this country "*A Hard Road to Glory*", after finding no definitive work on the subject,. This was his gift not just to African-Americans but also to all of us.

He died of AIDS, which he received as the result of a blood transfusion during an open-heart surgery. He died with the same class as he played the game of Tennis.

Jimmy Connors played as if every game was his last, with a wicked two-handed backhand that allowed him to have the best service return in the game. Connors began to play as a toddler and was raised to be a Tennis player. His mother was a teaching pro, and it has been said that Connors was taught by women to play men. Despite his smaller stature, Connors had an indomitable spirit that allowed him to outlast his opponents.

In 1974, he captured his first major when he won the Australian Open and then emerged victorious at Wimbledon and the U.S. Open. In both the US Open and Wimbledon, he dominated the legendary Ken Rosewell. Rosewell could only manage to win six games in six sets over these two tournaments. The French banned Connors because he played in the World Team Tennis (WTT) and French officials opposed the WTT and refused entry to any WTT player participation. Connors shot at a grand slam was dashed and at the age 21, he was at the height of this career. He even engaged in a highly publicized relationship with the women's best player, Chris Evert.

Connors not only astonished Tennis fans with his grittiness but, shocked them with his on court tactics. Unlike other past American champions just as Budge and Trabert, who acted the part of gentlemen—Connors would argue and on some occasions flip the middle finger to Tennis officials. After 1974, Connors would stay close to the number one ranking but would lose three Wimbledon finals to Arthur Ashe in 1975 and to Sweden's Bjorn Borg in 1977 and 78. During the late 70's and early 80's, Borg would win 11 majors, dominating the French Open and Wimbledon. Connors would end his career with 8 majors but would have losing records against John McEnroe, Bjorn Borg and Ivan Lendl. The one tournament where he could match his nearest competitors was the US Open where he beat both Lendl and Borg twice.

In 1991, Jimmy Connors would have one more great moment as he whipped the crowd into a frenzy and gutted his way through the semis in the US Open against younger opponents. He would lose in the semis but Stefan Edberg would win the tournament. Jim Courier ended Connors's run in the semifinals. The 1991 U.S. Open belonged to Jim Connors and at the end of his career, he finally won back the Tennis fans. Among those in the audience witnessing Connors last charge was a 9 year-old Andy Roddick. Jimmy Connors ended his career by winning more singles titles than any other player in the open era.

Controversial and always ready with the quote, **John McEnroe** was as colorful off the court as on. McEnroe would enrage Tennis officials with his version of vulgar behavior but no one ever doubted his ability or skill. McEnroe became America's best player in the early and mid 80's as he took over Connors place at the head of America's Tennis table. From 1979 through 1984, he won 4 US Opens and captured three Wimbledon's and added 70 more singles titles. While Jimmy Connors shied away from the Davis Cup, McEnroe led the United States to five Davis cup winners, the last being in 1992. He played Davis Cups for 13 years and still holds the record for most Davis Cup singles matches won.

McEnroe's patriotic feelings led him to regularly participate in Davis Cup and later he would be the Davis Cup Captain. (His brother, Patrick, replaced him as Davis Cup Captain.) While Connors would win one more major than McEnroe, McEnroe held the overall advantage over Jimmy Connors in head to head competition. For a five-year period in the early 80's, McEnroe was the world's best Tennis player though he would not win another major after 1984. His last final appearance in a major was the 1985 US Open. John McEnroe retired number three for most singles titles captured during the open era. Today, he is a commentator of the major Tennis events, and continuously promotes the game. McEnroe is as controversial in the booth as he was on the court, but the one thing that never left McEnroe was his love for the game.

Andre Agassi began the 90's as the hot property of Tennis. Championed as the new rebel, Agassi began his career as more flash than substance and saw his career go through its up and down. In the end, he would end up being one of America's greatest Tennis players. One of Agassi's biggest problems was that he played in the same era as Sampras, and these two great players faced each other five times in the finals of major tournaments with Sampras gaining the upper hand in four of five of these matches. If Agassi did not have to play Sampras, he would have won more majors.

Agassi won his first major in 1992 at the age of 22 years when he took Wimbledon, but his early career was marked with inconsistency. Just when it looked like Agassi was ready to take control of the Tennis world, he would take a step back and by 1997, Agassi was nearly out of the game. Ranked 141, he went back to the drawing board and did extensive conditioning to get himself back on top. From 1999 till the present, he won 5 majors and ranked among the top players. As he got older, he seemed to get better. Oh yea, he also participated on three Davis Cup winning teams.

Agassi never had the big booming serve but could place the ball where he wanted and his opponent usually did not. With one of the best returns in the game, Agassi used his smarts to beat the younger players and, he along with Sampras, led the golden age of American Tennis with both men over a 13 year period starting in 1990 winning nearly half of all majors and participating in 32 majors finals, including five against each other. He won every major at least once and presently has won eight majors in a career that still have some life left.

Pete Sampras was the quiet assassin, who would just go out and pound his opponent. If Pete had a weakness, he did not like to play on clay and never won the French Open. But in Tennis's premier events, the US Open and Wimbledon, Sampras dominated. Put Sampras on the hard court or grass and he conquered all. Wimbledon was his personal playground as he won seven of eight Wimbledon's between 1993 and 2000. On top of that, he won five US Opens including the 2002 final as he defeated his archrival Andre Agassi for the last time.

Sampras led the golden age of American Tennis with his skill. While Agassi was the media's favorite, Sampras was the superior player. Agassi had the popularity and was the more colorful character but Sampras let his Tennis do the talking. Agassi and Sampras were two of America's greatest, and Sampras was Tennis's best since the open era began when tennis players actually got paid for their efforts, and professionals were allowed to touch the hallowed grounds of Wimbledon and other tournaments. Sampras's 14 majors speak for themselves though Andre captured 8 majors and Jim Courier added 4 since 1990. Never before did America have so many great players at the same time. Sampras was the greatest. As he left the Tennis scene, his rival Agassi was still one of Tennis's best players.

Born in Czechoslovakia, **Ivan Lendl** did not officially become an American citizen until 1992 but it is worth discussing him here. Lendl did not win his first major until he was 24 but over the period of the next eleven years, Lendl appeared in at last one major finals and managed to capture 8 of them. It seemed that a major was never complete without Lendl in the finals and Lendl played himself into 19 finals. Lendl appeared in a record setting eight straight US Opens finals and his last major title was in 1990 as he was approaching the age of 30. Only Jimmy Connors would have won more singles titles in the open era than Lendl.

Summing it up

Andy Roddick and his fellow Americans have a tradition to uphold. Since Big Bill Tilden, American Tennis has seen its share of great players. Tilden combined theatrics with talent. Showing up once to a match in a Camel coat, Tilden showed a touch of arrogance with talent and set a standard both off and on the court that has yet to be matched.

Don Budge and Tony Trabert were the young gentlemen who played the game with class and talent. They allowed the game to speak for itself and it spoke plenty loud. They had the all around game, and there wasn't a surface they couldn't prevail on, but they played in an era when only amateurs could play on the big stage of the major tournaments. They shortened their amateur careers to make a living playing Tennis, but Tennis fans are still left with the following question—how many could they have won if there was an open era earlier?

Arthur Ashe demonstrated class and a social conscience whereas Connors and McEnroe would demonstrate vulgar behavior on the court along with their profligate skills. Ashe's class set a standard for what a Tennis player should be, but McEnroe and Connors showmanship would include the occasional exchanges with officials that resembled the WWF more than Tennis. They would entertain, and often their antics resembled the baseball manager who did the mandatory argument before being expelled.

Roddick plays like Sampras with a big booming serve and attacking style but he will excite the crowds like Connors, with his occasional bantering with judges and hand pumping. Roddick brings the enthusiasm of Connors, but is now looking for the steadiness of a Sampras or Agassi. Agassi and Sampras combined the class of past American players like Budge, along with their steady games. At their peak, they were a threat to win any title even late in their careers.

Agassi in the beginning of his career would date the hot chicks including Hollywood stars just as Brooke Shields, whom he married. He wore his hair long and advertised everything. Cannon featured Agassi as the new rebel, but now we see an older and wiser Agassi, who merely outthinks and out lasts his opponents. (And whose present wife, the great Steffi Graf was one of the great women's tennis players, if not the greatest. Certainly, she was the most dominant woman player of the open era.)

Roddick is still a young player at the age of 21 and certainly has a whole career ahead of him. Andre Agassi won his major at 22 years old-the same age Don Budge won his first major. Bill Tilden did not win his first until he was 27 years old, and he was still among the best even at the age of 37 years of age. Age is chronological but as Agassi has shown, age is not a factor when you play smart and stay in shape.

Roddick's game is based on power in an era where power is dominant. It is hard to predict a how a player's career will turn out, since many factors play a role. Injuries can shorten a career and Roddick certainly plays this game aggressively. Crashing upon hard courts leads to injuries, and this year alone Roddick sprained his ankle and wrist. Tennis elbows and shoulder injuries are potential injuries that are always close. The biggest enemy of a Tennis player is burnout. Agassi nearly played himself out of the game and Sampras's lack of productivity over the past two years of his career was as much due to lack of interest as age. As the 2002 Open demonstrated when Sampras played with desire, he was still one of the best. Many Tennis players have played this game their entire lives, beginning in their early teens. And eventually burn out happens. A tennis player must fight burn out.

Many foreigners have considered Roddick more style than substance and wondered, when will Roddick win the big one? Did Ivan Lendl face similar questions until he finally won his first major at the age of 24, or what about Rod Laver, who did not win his first major until he was past the age of 21? When discussing Borg, Borg was a star at an early age but by the time he was 27, he was no longer playing Tennis. Bill Tilden would not win his first title until he was 27, an age when Borg was relaxing finally in his native Sweden.

Roddick's place in history is yet to be written but he has the potential to join the other great Tennis stars and establish his own place in American Tennis history. Tennis players develop at different paces. Some like Bill Tilden did not begin to reach their potential until their late 20's, and Agassi won more majors after the age of 29 than he did before that age. So Roddick's future is bright and his only one major means nothing since there were many great players who never sat in the winner's circle until they were older than Roddick is today. This year showed the potential that is Roddick. Roddick won his first major.

Part Four: Journalist Round Table

Below are responses by some of Tennis's leading journalists, Jon Wertheim of Sports Illustrated, Brad Falkner of Tennis Week and James Buddell of Euro-sports, who provided a European perspective.

1. In the beginning of the year, did you forsee Roddick winning a major this year?

Jon Wertheim: "I'm not sure I necessarily foresaw it, but if you had said in January that Andy would win a slam by year's end, I wouldn't have been surprised. The guy did finish 2002 firmly embedded in the top 10 and anytime you can serve 140 mph, you give yourself a chance to win any match.

Brad Falkner: "Like most people I always felt that Andy's best chance, and first Slam would be the US Open. After Queens and Wimbledon this year, I feel that he will also win Wimbledon someday. I also believe that he will capture the Australian Open as well. The French will be difficult, but not impossible, as he has won multiple titles on Red Clay, and he is becoming much more patient."

James Buddell: Roddick is a Goran Ivanisevic or Richard Krajicek of the early 1990s, who has backup to his frontline game. He entertains and has the crowd on the edge of their seats in a way Jimmy Connors did throughout his career…. But for all the bravado, showmanship and determination to finish the 2002 season as the youngest American to finish the year in the Top Ten since 1992 on the back of four finals, Roddick appeared to have lost his way at the Grand Slam championships: where it counted…. Pete Sampras had schooled him in the 2002 U.S. Open quarterfinals and the big match temperament was lacking. A lack of maturity cost him at a time when his bandwagon was gaining momentum. His performance at the 2003 Australian Open didn't surprise me. He played to the crowd well through to the semi-finals and a marathon five set encounter with Moroccan Younes El Aynaoui in the last eight….The potential was there: the foundation blocks had been cast in stone and with greater emphasis placed on honing his main threats, Wimbledon and certainly the U.S. Open were where Andy Roddick could win and dominate in a style that would attract a new wave of tennis fans. This was to be his breakthrough year: the transition from young punk to Grand Slam winner.

2. What was Roddick's's key in his successful campaign this year?

Jon Wertheim: "The serve obviously is the foundation but his ground game (and patience) served him awfully well on the hard courts."

Brad Falkner: "After the El Aynauoi quarterfinal in Australia Roddick proved with out a doubt that he possesses the mental toughness to go far at the Slams. To me, he started to believe more in himself. This in turn leads to more confidence on the court."

James Buddell: "Too often players continue to employ their childhood or first professional coach for too long. So Roddick's decision to show the door to Tarik Benhabiles after his French Open loss was a bold move handled well."

3. How much credit do you give Gilbert and how much to Tarik?

Jon Wertheim: "Good question. Tarik obviously laid the foundation. Remember that Andy wasn't even a top junior when Tarik got him. But you have to give Brad Gilbert credit too for taking him the last mile. In retrospect, Andy seems to have played his hand awfully well. A baseball analogy: he let the starter stay in for eight innings and then went to the bullpen in the ninth inning to get the win."

Brad Falkner: "They both deserve heaps of credit. Despite his hiccup at the French, Roddick had been playing some solid tennis. I think that the coaching change came at exactly the right time and with the perfect guy. Gilbert was yearning for an opportunity like Roddick to come along. It was time for Andy to hear it from a fresh voice. Roddick has always given credit to Tarik and maintained that they still are close friends."

James Buddell: "Tarik is a Nick Bollettieri to an Andre Agassi, a man who pressed upon Roddick's consciousness that to simply have a U.S. college scholarship career was not enough…He put together the nuts and bolts: the weapons needed to succeed in the professional game and a fitness regime that saw Roddick's bulk-up in weight in his three years on tour…Brad Gilbert tinkered and polished the machine from the indoor courts of Queen's Club onto the summer form that culminated in a Wimbledon semi-final, back-to-back Masters Series wins and the adulation of millions in New York barely ten weeks later…Gilbert installed the belief that to reach the second week of a Grand Slam tournament was not enough. To remain a challenger on the final day was what counted for a player searching for his own slice of history…Gilbert tightened his serve and cut the unforced errors on his forehand wing in half. He wallpapered the cracks that appeared on Roddick's backhand side, adjusting Roddick's grip and footwork enough to make opponents think twice about hitting a short ball to his 'weaker' side...In the same way as Roger Federer gave praise to Peter Carter—who died last year in a car accident—after the Wimbledon final, Roddick remembered Benhabiles contribution and insistence in 2001 that "two years from now he is going to be ready to do big things on tour."

4. What did you find to be Tarik's strength as a coach?

Jon Wertheim: "I think tennis coaching tends to get overanalyzed. Oftentimes the most important function a coach can serve is just being a buddy, a confidante to the player who makes life on tour comfortable and buffers the highs and lows. I think Tarik's strength—beyond the tennis—was helping oversee a smooth transition from juniors to the pros."

Brad Falkner: "Hard for me to answer, as I never spoke to him or watched a match at his side. My guess is that he helped A-Rod to stay focused and was like a father to him, especially on the road."

James Buddell: "Benhabiles has the ability to develop a fledging career onto the track for a successful professional career. While the Frenchman reached a career-high 29th in the world, flirting with the top earners, albeit briefly, much of his philosophy as a player was transferred to Roddick, who gainfully employed him in June 1999. Fitness played a big part in pre-match preparation of both Benhabiles the player, and as coach...His ability lies in breaking a player down in his biomechanics of movement on court and the conservation of energy between shots. When Roddick transferred allegiances to Brad Gilbert in June 2003, the partnership had run its course. Benhabiles has taken Roddick through the dying embers of his successful junior career through the pitfalls of his early professional days. The building blocks were in place, but the consistency needed improving, the rough edges needed to be polished."

5. The same question about Gilbert?

Jon Wertheim: "As for Gilbert, people think he's this masterful technical coach. It's the opposite: he simplifies the tennis and really filled Andy with positive thoughts. It's not as though he has made major adjustments to Andy's strokes and retooled his serve."

Brad Falkner: "One of his greatest strengths is his ability to scout other players. He knows how you should play almost every player out there. He has gotten Andy to ditch the visor and get his emotions under control. He is teaching Andy to be a much smarter player. He has him hitting a wider variety of serves, and has gotten Roddick to serve and volley more often. The bond between these two is strong. They have so much in common, they love to rap about sports and music."

James Buddell: "Gilbert realizes that to become a professional you have to be more than talented and for this reason stresses the implications upon his charges of a honed mental approach. By treating every point as an advantage point and believing that you have one-serve with which to play and win a match he breaks a difficult game to learn well into an acute science. "These are just two of the favorite ploys used by the 42-year-old in order to motivate a player. Considered a hard taskmaster who takes his role as professionally as he expects his player to, he has an insatiable appetite to learn and contrive new approaches to upsetting the form-horses of the ATP tour…if ever the United States appointed him as their Davis Cup captain, the legendary records of coaches Harry Hopman, Perry T. Jones and Neale Fraser may be closely examined."

6. Where did Roddick made his biggest improvement?

Jon Wertheim: "His backhand."

Brad Falkner: "Biggest improvement—concentration. He has learned to not let his emotions drain valuable energy from him. He has added a solid one-handed slice backhand. His approach shots have improved as well."

James Buddell: "As a professional's career develops the chances for improvement become magnified in light of the development of weapons, be it, the serve or forehand for example. In Roddick's case Gilbert has continued to build from existing foundations laid down by Benhabiles…the Nebraskan was prone to rush through games when facing difficult situations in matches. Although the familiar twitching and adjusting of cap, shorts and strings remain, the big-match nerves have all but vanished…Roddick's biggest improvement has come in the placement and control on his serve—no longer hitting double faults—with a first serve percentage finding court rocketing upwards."

Having taken the bold decision to sign Brad Gilbert as coach, Roddick had opened up a new world of possibilities.

In the same way as Sampras began to organize his schedule around the four Grand Slam championships, the 21-year-old had bridged the gap of tour journeyman to majors winner.

Benhabiles would have helped him win a couple of U.S. Open titles, but now with 42-year-old Gilbert, a former world number four on board the prospect of winning a coveted Wimbledon singles crown looks likely.

Four-to-six Slams looks a fair bet.

7. Which areas does Roddick still need improvement in?

Jon Wertheim: "What's scary is that he can probably improve 5-10 percent in everything. The backhand pass is a specific shot he could upgrade."

Brad Falkner: "Roddick should work on his agility and foot speed. This will pay dividends on his serve and volley game. He can improve his return of serve and volley."

James Buddell: With the best serve in the game, offering opponents very little chance to latch onto a service return, Roddick shows tremendous reluctance to advance to the net…More often than not all his opponent can do is block the serve, using Roddick's pace thus floating the return back down the middle of the court. This glitch was in evidence during the Cincinnati Masters Series final against friend and compatriot Mardy Fish…while Gilbert has installed a greater consistency, both technically and mentally to his game, Roddick remains susceptible to being caught flat-footed on his backhand swing…Often players' catch the Nebraskan with 'kicked' serves out wide on the advantage court to his backhand, as the nature of his backhand relies heavily on a flatter impact in comparison to the heavy topspin generated by his forehand….In this instance you often find him too far from the ball upon impact and this is why he shanks (frames) out to all corners of the stadium arena.

8. Name in your opinion Roddick's biggest rivals. What are their strengths and weaknesses relative to Andy's.

Jon Wertheim: "Federer has more innate talent and is a smoother player. When he's on (as he was at Wimbledon) he'll give Andy fits. When he's not (which is often) Andy is mentally stronger and probably has a better serve. Hewitt, though he is slipping, probably qualifies as a rival. He competes (used to anyway) better than Roddick and is an opponent that demands patience (not Andy's strong suit.) on the one hand, Andy has the ability to simply overpower Hewitt. As a rule I think Andy will always beat the Srichaphans and the Philippoussises, (players who essentially play his power game, just not as well.) He will be challenged by the steady and quick baseliners, (Coria, Ferrero, Hewitt, Scheuttler, Nalbandian) who will get a lot of balls back.

Brad Falkner: "Agassi, Federer, Nalbandian, and Fish. Ferrerro and Hewitt hopefully in the future. One of the biggest problems in tennis is the lack of rivalries. Roddick has not played Hewitt since their classic 2001 quarterfinals clash."

James Buddell: "Federer is an all-court player, who on any given day can blow aside opponents with his variety and consistency. While Roddick may be developing fearsome weapons of his own, the pair has adopted fuller schedules this year the chances of being burnt-out are always there…Federer has all the shots, but his inconsistency is his consistency, so the chances of him dining at tennis's top table could prevent him from a more permanent place…but this I'm sure will be one of the main rivalries in Roddick's career."

In winning Roland Garros and reaching the U.S. Open finals, Ferrero proved to worldwide audiences that the current crop of the Spanish Armada is the most talented since Manuel Santana and Orantes…The current world number one had improved his serve and often catches opponents with his hard groundstrokes and deft drop shot touches. Roddick may have dealt with him in New York, but the 23-year-old wasn't allowed to play. The American would do well to look at Ferrero's willingness to attack the short ball and his excellent hands at the net."

The standard bearer at the top of the game for two years, Hewitt is still only a 22-year-old. But problems with the ATP, coaches and a loss of form this year hardly fuels any expectation that the Australian will be back challenging at the majors soon…the speed around the court and determination has been tempered and Hewitt's on-going problems have opened the door for his rivals…Hewitt's strength is his ability to counter tight situations with fearsome warnings of sheer power in a game suited to fast courts. His serve has improved but it is his consistency that has won him two Grand Slams. In the same way as Michael Chang fell-away at the top of the rankings in 1998 when his speed deserted him, so too the Australian could find that his game is brushed aside in the next couple of years.

Argentina's best player since Guillermo Vilas, Nalbandian is starting to prove that his Wimbledon final of 2002 is no fluke…The 21-year-old has a burgeoning all-court game, centered on a classy backhand that has the ability to find the lines with regular monotony. Nalbandian needs to improve his serve if he wants to secure a consistent top five end-of-season ranking, but shows his court craft, in the same way as Juan Carlos Ferrero. If Roddick's game is slightly wayward on any given day Nalbandian will capitalize on the glitch and maximize his chances of winning.

If Marat Safin (Russia) were to recover from his injury agony of 2003 and regain the kind of form that won him the 2000 U.S. Open title and the tag of 'the new Sampras' as a teenager, then he could thwart Roddick, Federer and Ferrero in the Grand Slam cauldron for years to come. Once against the mental side of a game that looks so easy to him has never been fully harnessed by his coaches, and for this reason only if he ends his career as a one-Slam wonder it'll be the biggest waste of talent for years.

Afterword

The whole country, and probably the whole world, has been preparing for Andy Roddick to be the Superstar he now is ever since his first majors run at the US Open in 2001. He's had the looks, the game, the charisma, and all the hype a superstar can possibly have without being a true Superstar with a Grand Slam Win. Therefore, the second he won the US Open, it was as if everything was in place to introduce to the world Andy Roddick, the Superstar Athlete, Grand Slam Champion. That is why it was no surprise to see Andy gracing the sets of Letterman, Regis, MTV, ESPN, CNN and be on the cover of every major publication including NY Times and Sports Illustrated immediately following his victory Sunday.

The fact is now that he has won the US OPEN, he is America's newest Rock star, and as we have grown to learn, he is more than ready to accept that role. His wit, charm and spontaneity are perfect while being interviewed, and when you throw in his polished looks and trendy style, Andy is the perfect blueprint for celebrity of your life, and that is the mark of a champion.

To be honest, I think the tennis public has known for about 5 weeks leading up to the U.S. Open that Andy is a legitimate champion on the same level as Federer, Hewitt and Ferrero. His convincing form day in and day out on the hard courts in Indianapolis, Washington, Montreal and Cincinnati answered every question that anyone had about his ability to compete at the highest of levels. The fact is in order to beat him you have to play the match the way he won all those matches this summer, he had to play a great deal and that is mentally and physically exhausting. Would his mind and body hold up for the 7 matches of 3 out of 5 sets? That's what makes this victory even that much more amazing.

In fact, on Tuesday, in speaking to another tennis player, he said it looked like he could have played another grand slam event starting Monday.

Therefore the tennis public is not surprised, but probably more relieved that we can finally appropriate him the status that he has earned, the status that we all want him to have. He is the people's champion, now and probably for a long time.

Scot Hirschfield, SFX, September 10, 2003

About the Authors

Tom Donelson has enjoyed nearly a quarter century of writing various columns on issues ranging from economics and foreign affairs to sporting events. As an author, he has authored four other books, *Economics 101 And Other Thoughts*, *Viewing Boxing From Ringside*, *More Tales From Ringside* (Co-Authored with Frank Lotierzo) and *Empire of Liberty*.

Over the last two decades, Tom has given numerous lectures on public policy and currently acts as a consultant and writer in addition to running his own publishing company, Donelson Research and Publishing.

Bethany Donelson—Ms. Donelson is presently attending the University of Iowa but has written about Men's Tennis for various online sites for the past two years. She is part of the managerial team of the website *Roddick n Roll*, and presently contributes to the new online site *Menstennisworld.com*.

Special Offer

As a way of saying thanks for buying this book, we offer you a FREE trial of Tennis Celebs, the newsletter that reports on the rich and famous tennis people.

To get your FREE copy, e-mail bob@tenniscelebs.com.

0-595-30785-X

Printed in the United Kingdom
by Lightning Source UK Ltd.
105293UKS00002B/134